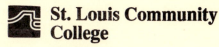

THE CASE AGAINST SCHOOL CHOICE

THE CASE AGAINST SCHOOL CHOICE

Politics, Markets, and Fools

Kevin B. Smith

Kenneth J. Meier

M.E. Sharpe
Armonk, New York
London, England

Library of Congress Cataloging-in-Publication Data

Smith, Kevin B., 1963–
The case against school choice : politics, markets, and fools /
Kevin B. Smith and Kenneth J. Meier.
p.   cm.
Includes bibliographical references and index.
ISBN 1-56324-519-1 (alk. paper). — ISBN 1-56324-520-5 (pbk. : alk. paper)
1. School choice—Wisconsin—Milwaukee—Case studies.
I. Meier, Kenneth J., 1950–   . II. Title
LB1027.9.S656   1995
371´.01—dc20   94-33509
CIP

Printed in the United States of America

The paper used in this publication meets the minimum requirements of
American National Standard for Information Sciences—
Permanence of Paper for Printed Library Materials,
ANSI Z 39.48-1984.

MV (c)   10   9   8   7   6   5   4   3   2   1
MV (p)   10   9   8   7   6   5   4   3   2   1

To Kelly and C.C.

——————— Contents ———————

———— List of Tables ————

——— Preface ———

During the past decade school choice has emerged as a major focus of the education reform movement. Promising solutions to seemingly intractable problems, choice has been enthusiastically championed within and outside the education community. Most of these promises remain unfulfilled, and the ability of the education marketplace to rescue the nation's education system remains a theoretical rather than an empirical argument.

The purpose of this book is not to add to the impassioned ideological essays that are the main source of ammunition for the choice debate. We take the central theory of school choice, draw a list of testable hypotheses from that theory, and put those hypotheses to the empirical acid test. Our conclusions are controversial, and we would not be so disingenuous as to claim that we are merely humble scientists in search of truth who jettisoned the baggage of our own opinions. Still, while controversial, our findings are the result of a series of careful and objective research projects—many revealed here for the first time—and not the dogma of our own, or anybody else's, ideology. We conclude that the theory providing the rationale for school choice simply does not fit with reality. Instead of being a panacea, school choice has the potential to affect adversely the overall performance of America's education system.

Although both of us are data-oriented social scientists, we have attempted to make this book as accessible as possible. All the results of our more sophisticated statistical analyses are included in an appendix. We do not want to limit our audience to those with a certain level of expertise in number crunching. Accordingly, the body of the book can be read without reference to these tables and we hope will be informative reading for undergraduates, policymakers, and interested lay persons.

We begin our undertaking in chapter one by venturing into the classroom and the district offices of public, private, and parochial schools. We ask students and school officials what they believe to be wrong with the education system and how they would go about correcting such deficiencies. Chapter two examines the nature of the educational "crisis," how it has been exaggerated, and the various responses to the perception of decline. Chapter three examines the intellectual and theoretical support of school choice; and from the most persuasive universal theory, a list of testable hypotheses and counterhypotheses. Chapter four reports an initial test of these hypotheses on a district level, and chapter five expands this test to concentrate on the probable outcomes of a competitive education marketplace. Chapter six begins our test of state-level education policy, and chapter seven expands this into a comprehensive analysis of the reform movement of the 1980s. Chapter eight examines choice from an international perspective, taking the primary global economic competitors of the United States and identifying the distinguishing characteristics of their education systems. Chapter nine attempts to bring together all the strands of our research into a cohesive explanation of where and why the main arguments supporting school choice have failed. The Epilogue concludes the book by bringing us back to where we started—the classroom and the opinions of those who will be most affected by the outcomes of education reform.

Such an extensive project is rarely the product of two people's labor. We would like to thank the participants of various conference panels and the anonymous reviewers at various academic journals, who provided thoughtful criticism and guidance for the embryonic beginnings of this research. We would like to thank all those who were generous enough to share their time, their opinions, or their data. We would like to thank our wives, who for reasons unknown put up with us while we ignore them for projects such as this. While credit is rightly shared, error must be assigned to a single source—Paul Sabatier. For reasons shrouded in mystery, Paul has traditionally been assigned blame for all of Ken's mistakes. As both authors believe this to be a profitable and worthy arrangement, Paul now gets the blame for Kevin's boo-boos as well.

Kevin B. Smith
Kenneth J. Meier

One

The Hobgoblins of Education Policy

The whole aim of practical politics is to keep the populace alarmed (and hence clamorous to be led to safety) by menacing it with an endless series of hobgoblins, all of them imaginary.

—H.L. Mencken

One of the most widely cited examples of America's education decline is a comparison of the top ten problems in public schools in the 1940s and the 1980s. In the 1940s the list was headed by talking, chewing gum, making noise, running in the halls, and cutting in line. In the 1980s these infractions had been replaced by drug and alcohol abuse, pregnancy, suicide, and rape.

As an example of the erosion of the nation's education infrastructure, the list has been used by conservatives and liberals alike. Former Secretary of Education William Bennett has quoted the list in his writings, as has columnist Anna Quindlen. The *Wall Street Journal* has printed the list, citing the *Congressional Quarterly Researcher* as a source. Former Surgeon General Joycelyn Elders used the list to promote the need for social programs. The list is not only widely quoted but also widely believed. It represents what much of the public perceives to be true about the public school system and its steady decline. This list is considered official, is largely unquestioned, and is held as proof incontrovertible of the decline of America's schools in the postwar era. But few realize that the list is based on one man's opinions, rather than any objective survey.

The list originated, not as social science or journalism, but as a rhetorical salvo from T. Cullen Davis, a born-again Christian and high-profile critic of public schools. He wrote the list based on his own views of what he thought was wrong with today's schools, compared with schools during his days as a student, and used it to further his fundamentalist-based campaign against public schools. The list has since evolved into treasured folklore presented as truth. More scientific polls—largely ignored in the education debate—indicate that the biggest problems faced in classrooms are discipline and safety and that these have remained largely unchanged. The creation and perpetuation of the school-list myth have been closely examined in a 1994 essay by Barry O'Neill.[1] He concludes that the list—there are several versions—represents a "collective moan of anxiety over the gap between ideals and reality" (O'Neill 1994, 49). It also demonstrates how readily myth can replace reality in the volatile arena of public education.

Identifying and agreeing on educational problems—let alone solutions—is very difficult, but that does not stop people from trying. If facts are not available, or do not fit ideological preconceptions, they are ignored or, as in the case of the school lists, simply made up. Any number of scholars, politicians, and a legion of self-described education "experts" have joined the fray of the education debate, quoting highly subjective "evidence" such as the school list to support their positions. Barricaded behind thick walls of ideology, views limited by selective perceptions, and armed with carelessly handled reports and studies, many participants in the education debate seem to be more intent on defending folklore than exploring reality.

At the center of the education debate is a reform effort that emerged from the 1980s with growing strength: school choice. Depending on who is asked, school choice is either the savior of America's decaying education system or another myth on a par with the school list that is just as false and much more dangerous. The idea behind school choice is to create an education marketplace where students or parents could choose school services, and their educational tax dollars would be allocated accordingly. Students will demand higher educational quality, and in the name of financial and institutional survival, schools will supply the same. To back this claim, there is theory, ideology, and even an empirical study or two.

The purpose of this book is an objective analysis of school choice. But before we started examining policy and crunching numbers, we thought it would be good to ground ourselves in reality by venturing into nearby classrooms. As the rhetoric demonstrates, diagnoses of the problems with schools and prescriptions to cure them are often not shared by those who work and study in the nation's elementary and secondary education system. We did not want to start by listening to the stories told by the hobgoblins of ideology. Instead of telling students and officials what their problems were and how they could address these deficiencies, we decided to begin by asking them what, if anything, they thought was wrong.

The Milwaukee metropolitan area contains a wide variety of secondary and elementary education systems. These include a large urban school system, private and parochial schools, and a network of modern suburban school districts. In addition to these traditional schools, Milwaukee has one of the nation's first experimental school choice programs and a court-ordered desegregation plan—Chapter 220—that buses mostly inner-city blacks and suburban whites across traditional demographic boundaries.[2] Between January and May of 1994 we conducted a series of interviews with students, administrators, and parents drawn from this mosaic of education. We asked them to describe their education experience, what they thought of their schools, what could be done to improve them, and whether they thought being granted the right to attend any school they chose would improve their academic performance or enhance their educational experience. What follows are some of their answers.

Michael, Graduate, Arrowhead High School

Michael,[3] nineteen, recently graduated from Arrowhead High School, part of the Hartland-Arrowhead School District on the western reaches of the Milwaukee suburbs. He is a now a college freshman who takes his studies seriously. He devoted considerable time to thinking about and responding to questions on improving education and went so far as to develop a list of what he believed to be feasible policy options to improve schools. Someone should be paying attention to making changes in school, he said, and they should be taking it seriously.

Michael's student career stretches well beyond the Arrowhead district. With family moves and shifting education objectives, Michael has experienced both parochial and public schools and has attended classes in the inner city and in suburbia. Much of his early education was in Catholic schools, which he gives mixed marks. He said Catholic schools offered discipline and "certainly made me more civilized," but did not have the educational richness or opportunities of public schools.

From ninth through eleventh grades he attended Rufus King High, part of Milwaukee Public Schools (MPS). Like many urban schools, MPS has a résumé of depressing statistics. In 1993 grades averaged a D+, the dropout rate for African Americans neared 20 percent, and in seven of its fifteen high schools more than half of the ninth grade flunked basic algebra.[4] Rufus King, however, is the district's college prep high school, and Michael says it offered a good education with a diverse curriculum, challenging courses, and good teachers. People took academics seriously at Rufus King because that was the main focus.

In his senior year, Michael transferred to Arrowhead. "Arrowhead had everything a person could want in a high school," he said. "Good teachers, well educated and caring. Well financed, clean, little crime." While the school was high quality, he felt most students did not want to take advantage of the opportunity: "Being at Arrowhead was like being at a big mall—it was safe, but it wasn't serious."

Michael took several days to compile his fifteen suggestions on how to improve schools. Leading the list were equalization of funding for schools and improvement of the living conditions for inner-city families. Much of the remainder dealt with parental involvement and student responsibility. Number three on his list was "video cameras in classrooms." Number four was "educate parents on helping their children." Number five was "parents who do not attempt to help children should be punished. Possibly fined." Number ten was "problem students should not be able to obtain a driver's license."

Prompted to explain his suggestions, Michael said it was the students and not the schools that interfered with the learning process. Society's responsibility should be to provide decent schools and a chance to attend them. After that, the onus of education falls on parents and students. From his experience, he judged parents and students to be failing their end of the education contract. Parents are rarely involved in school or their children's education, and students pick up these indifferent attitudes toward education. A significant minority of students were disruptive, violent, or simply failed to show up (metal detectors and more truant officers also made his list). If you want to improve education, Michael said, that is where you should start.

School choice did not make his list. Asked why, Michael said it would not solve the problems his list was designed to address. But he was attracted to the idea of choice if it would allow students to avoid unsafe schools. Choice, however, should be a privilege denied to violent students.

John Norris, Superintendent of Milwaukee
Catholic Schools

John Norris is the titular head of Catholic schools in the Archdiocese of Milwaukee. His spacious office is in the large, modern building on the city's south side that serves as administrative headquarters for archdiocesan operations. He is friendly and accommodating to visitors and quickly warms to the subject of how to improve education. Norris has little hesitation in identifying what has gone wrong with the nation's education system or how to correct it. As he puts it, "We didn't have all these problems when religion was taught in schools."

Schools, Norris says, should be about more than reading, writing, and 'rithmetic. Schools should aid and assist parents in developing the whole child, and that includes teaching values. It is this focus, Norris believes, that provides Catholic schools with their strength.

Norris says there are several reasons for the well-documented academic success of Catholic school students. It begins with parents. "We can only build upon what's there," he says. While there are no formal requirements for enrolling in Milwaukee's Catholic schools, Norris says there may be something of a natural selection process for the student body. "Parents who are willing to make the investment" in their children's education and values are those who find their way to Catholic schools. A successful student often begins with a concerned parent.

Norris also attributes part of Catholic school success to the decentralized system. Although some archdioceses require approval of textbooks, and all Catholic schools have a degree of religious focus, the schools in Milwaukee are basically free to do as they please. Curriculum, hiring and firing, and most budget matters are decided at the local level.

And this is as it should be, says Norris. Catholic schools historically have strong ties to the neighborhood or parish they serve, where money is raised and where families may have traditions of attendance.

Norris says Catholic schools have no real advantages over public schools in the areas of curriculum or facilities. "In many ways our academic programs are skin and bone compared to public schools. There aren't a lot of frills."

Norris strongly favors school choice. He says any choice program should allow students to choose parochial schools and should allow their education tax dollars to follow them. "If parochial schools are shut out of choice, it's not choice," says Norris. He believes schools that emphasize values and offer religion-based education will be attractive to many parents, who are the key to educational success. "We have to get that parental investment."

Tony, Student, Hayes Alternative School (MPS)

Tony is an outgoing eighth grader who is constantly in motion. During an interview he punctuates his speech with gestures, taps his feet, and becomes impatient with the interviewer when the questions bore him. He comes from a poor, inner-city, single-parent family and, by his own admission, has an indifferent attitude toward the MPS schools he has attended. But he is concerned that this attitude is being emulated by his brother. "I flunked one grade and now my brother's doing it. I don't know what he's thinking."

Tony admits to sometimes having an attitude problem. Once given a three-day suspension for disruptive behavior, he subsequently skipped school for three weeks. "I got a short temper. Sometimes I just skip out and walk around town all day." Asked what it would take to get him back in the classroom and interested in his education, he shrugs and says, "I don't know."

Asked how he would improve education, he responds by saying better teachers and better textbooks. Especially better teachers. "Some of the rules they have are just stupid, and some teachers are plain crazy." He is unsure, however, how schools can attract better teachers or even what makes a better teacher. Informed about teacher certification programs, he becomes enthusiastic about the idea. He likes the notion of teachers taking tests.

Tony is indifferent to the notion of choice, and is highly skeptical of any system that depends on greater parental involvement. "My mother doesn't care," he says. Tony's efforts to cut the interview short succeed.

Mr. Galley's Sixth Period Physics Class, St. Joan Antida Catholic High School

The seniors in Brian Galley's sixth period physics class are articulate and inquisitive. The eighteen female students—St. Joan Antida is a single-sex institution—are eager to grapple with the problem of improving education. They politely raise their hands and deliver their opinions in thoughtful monologues that are quickly dissected by their classmates.

After ten minutes of this sort of discussion, several areas of consensus are agreed upon. Secondary and elementary education can benefit from a disciplined environment, small class size, and an emphasis on early education. Attracting good teachers is considered critical. "Teachers play the most important role in the classroom," says one. "A good student can be wasted with a bad teacher," says another. There is unanimous agreement that parental involvement and interest are critical to academic success.

The class is intrigued by the idea of school choice. They are enthusiastic, but see Milwaukee's experimental program (which proscribes religious schools) as too limited. Parochial and single-sex institutions should be a part of any choice plan. Several students emphasize the point that single-sex education is a great benefit to girls and should be given greater consideration in any education reform.

Also expressed is a general disdain of standardized testing to judge education quality or achievement. Asked how people should judge whether students and schools are working or improving, there is a slight pause before a student toward the back of the class raises her hand. "Judge us for who we are, not what the SATs say we are," she says.

Helen, Graduate, Rufus King High School (MPS)

Helen just graduated from Rufus King after spending her entire grade school career in MPS schools. She considers herself lucky to have attended the flagship MPS school because enrollment is based on a lottery system, and hers was an eleventh-hour acceptance.[5] Originally she had been slotted to attend Vincent High—a school with a much less desirable reputation. "The thought of going to Vincent was scary, to say the least. All I'd heard about was the violence there, the big-time gang stuff."

Rufus King was different. "It was the magnet school, for the college bound . . . if you went there, people assumed you were a brain." She says reputation and attitude played a big role in the direction of the school. "We were always told we were the cream of the crop." Helen says one of the best things about her alma mater was the diversity of classes it offered for her to choose from.

In another sense, choice was nonexistent. "I'm from the inner city and I wanted choice, I wanted to be able to choose the school I went to. I sure didn't like the one they were going to send me to." Helen said the best way to improve the education system would be to have more schools like Rufus King and give students the option of getting out of schools like Vincent. The obvious quality gap between schools meant some people were getting shortchanged on their educations. "I just don't like the idea of good schools and bad schools. There should be just good schools."

The only problem she saw with school choice was that it was not necessarily the school that created the problems she saw and feared at Vincent. It was the students—and if they all chose to leave Vincent for another school, the problem would be relocated, not solved. Some would have to be left behind. Who? Helen said she did not have an answer to the question.

She also said that Rufus King, even though it was the "brainy" school, had its share of problems. While she was there, the school went through three principals in four years and the administration was seen as providing little direction or control. Despite being the cream of the crop, the student body also exhibited its share of problems. There were a lot of pregnancies, a few disruptive attitudes. Helen herself was something of an oddity—she was one of only a handful of people she knew at school who had parents who were still together.

Kameron, Student, Hamilton High School

Kameron is an inner-city resident who takes a forty-minute commute to get to school. He is bused to the suburban Hamilton School District as part of the Chapter 220 desegregation program. An articulate and thoughtful tenth grader, Kameron is also angry. He believes he has found a better education opportunity in the suburbs, but that opportunity is being at least partially spoiled by racial tensions with local students. "You're labeled as a 220 kid, you're looked down upon. People make certain assumptions about you, none of them nice."

Still, despite the problems, he believes in the 220 program as a way to offer inner-city students a better education. "The 220 program is good, and it should be bigger. There should be more people brought out here." Overall, he rates his education as high quality and has praise for his teachers and the curriculum at Hamilton. He insists there are problems, but is vague about the details. Pressed about how he would go about improving his education, he repeatedly returns to the racial question and to the paradox of suburban whites who are simultaneously prejudiced against inner-city blacks yet attracted to the outlaw stereotype. "You have a lot of white kids who are infatuated with the ghetto lifestyle. We call them 'wiggers.' They're idiots. If you live that life, like I've had to, it's not something you want to emulate."

Kameron says it would not be fair to characterize Hamilton based on racial tensions and that he is more than content to stay and graduate. He much prefers Hamilton to the Catholic schools he previously attended. "You have more choice in public schools, you didn't get to choose your curriculum in Catholic school. You took what you were given."

He is initially attracted to school choice and talks enthusiastically about being able to opt out of a dangerous inner-city school. His initial support begins to wane as he identifies some potential outcomes of a choice system. "Choice would segregate," he says. That will not help what he perceives to be the main problem with his education environment—racism. "If you really want to improve everything, their attitudes have to change. Really change."

Dan, Student, Elmbrook High School and James Madison High School

Dan is an easygoing individual with a passion for music. During most of his classes a guitar case is propped against his desk, and he is more likely to be seen carrying his instrument than his books in the halls. He laughs easily, and he prefers to concentrate on problems with chord progressions rather than education policy.

For one high school semester Dan transferred from the safe and wealthy suburban Elmbrook School District to James Madison High in Milwaukee. It was an experience he would rather not repeat. He says two differences represented the gulf between the suburban and the inner-city education experience. One was attitude. There were many students at James Madison who simply ignored their education. They were disrespectful to teachers or were simply tuned out. The second difference was in the architecture. "It was strange to come from a suburban school to an inner-city school. At Madison there were security guards, metal detectors, wire mesh on the windows, and these buzzers on the doors. The buzzers locked the doors, so when you were in, you were in. It was weird." He still wonders if all the security precautions were to keep others out or students in.

As a resident of a suburban school district, Dan had a choice after his semester at Madison and he exercised it. He opted out and went back to Elmbrook.

Vicente Castellanos, Principal, Bruce Guadalupe Community School

Bruce Guadalupe Community School is housed in a modern, airy building that has few frills but all the basics. Castellanos's office sits just off the main entrances and is functional rather than comfortable. To a visitor there is nothing that immediately identifies Bruce Guadalupe as part of one of the more radical education experiments operating in the nation. Nearly 50 percent of the school's more than three hundred students are school choice students. Here is an opportunity to gauge how a real-life choice program matches its abstract ideal.

The Milwaukee Parental Choice Program allows a limited number of lower-income students in the MPS system to attend private schools. The participating private schools receive the roughly $2,500 per student in state funds that would normally be given to MPS in lieu of tuition. Castellanos firmly believes that the choice program of which Bruce Guadalupe is a part has proven itself successful and should be expanded. "Choice works," he says.

Many choice parents with children at Bruce Guadalupe agree with Castellanos's assessment. The primary differences between Bruce Guadalupe and the MPS institutions that school choice students would otherwise attend are smaller student-teacher ratios, the complete absence of gang-related or violence problems, a dress code, and an insistence on parental involvement.[6] Parents must sign a contract committing them to thirty hours of volunteer work for the school as a condition of their child's enrollment. Castellanos says that during a typical school year, parents will put in more than 6,200 hours of volunteer work.

This emphasis on the whole family—not just the individual student—helps make Bruce Guadalupe unique. "Education is not just schools, you have to bring parents, whole families into the picture,"

Castellanos says. He says the choice program has offered many of Bruce Guadalupe's students an education opportunity they may have missed by attending public schools, and he has evidence to back such a claim. Besides high levels of parental satisfaction, the number of Bruce Guadalupe school choice students who score above the 50th percentile on the Iowa Test of Basic Skills has improved in both reading and math. After graduating from Bruce Guadalupe, many of the school choice students go on to enroll in some of the most prestigious public and private college prep schools in the area. There is a waiting list of more than seventy families trying to enroll children in Bruce Guadalupe under the choice program. Castellanos is prevented from admitting them in large part because under current legislation choice students are not allowed to exceed 49 percent of total enrollment.

Despite his enthusiasm for choice, Castellanos has some reservations. One of the problems that has surfaced since Bruce Guadalupe entered the choice program is a high turnover of students. Fully 10 percent of the choice student population dropped out in the first six weeks of the spring 1994 semester. Such a high turnover creates obvious problems with stability and raises questions about the validity of annual test results. It is hard to credit a school with improving scores if different students are taking the test each year.

Castellanos says there are two main contributing factors to the high rate of turnover: transportation and lack of parental involvement. There are no provisions to transport school choice students to the school they enroll in, and this obviously creates burdens on a low-income family. Some parents simply seem to lose interest. Choice, Castellanos readily admits, works best for families with parents who are willing to make a commitment to education.

Castellanos also does not see choice as being able to eliminate large centralized institutions like MPS. Because of their size they can provide services that smaller private schools such as Bruce Guadalupe cannot. For example, one choice student at Bruce Guadalupe was recently returned to MPS because he needed a speech therapist. MPS can provide those services, but for Bruce Guadalupe it would be too expensive. While remaining committed to the choice ideal, Castellanos says it offers an addition to, rather than a replacement of, the existing public school system. "[Choice] can help up to a certain percentage of students . . . a high percentage. But it's not a panacea." Success is predicated on high levels of family involvement, and "some families just don't participate."

Castellanos says choice programs can help large urban districts such as MPS by helping to provide a variety of high-quality education services. Private schools participating in choice programs should be partners with public schools in the education enterprise, not competitors. "I certainly don't see choice as a threat to public schools," he says.

Saundra Garza, Choice Parent

Saundra Garza is a single mother who lives and works right in the heart of Milwaukee's Hispanic community, just south of city center. She could not afford to pay private school tuition for her daughter, Ashley, and did not want to send her to a public school. The Milwaukee choice program, which sends poor inner-city children to private schools with taxpayer money, was the answer to her dilemma. Ashley, who recently entered the first grade, attends Bruce Guadalupe Community School. Saundra is a relentless booster of the choice program and believes it should be expanded.

She has a low opinion of public schools. "In public schools you have too many students in a class, too many teachers who are only there for a paycheck . . . as a parent I'm concerned that my kid is in a school, not a baby-sitting facility," she says. Although Saundra did attend public schools for a time, her family mostly opted for Catholic or private schools. Her recommendation for improving education is simple: let more public school students attend the same kind of Catholic and private schools.

Still, she also believes school choice has its limits. There is still a role for a large, centralized institution such as MPS, she says, to deal with special education students and others with needs that small schools cannot cope with. She also believes the choice option is probably wasted if parents are not committed to their children's education. "If the parents aren't interested, then there's no point in sending their kids to a choice school." Saundra has no problem in making this commitment. "I would do just about anything for my child's education," she says.

Conclusion

Although by no means random, the varying views presented here on education and school choice offer some useful insights. The first of these is that school choice has inherent positive connotations. Asked whether individuals should have the right to the education services of their own choosing, most people say yes.

But as soon as choice shifts from an abstract notion to a concrete policy proposal, the almost uniformly positive appraisal begins to break down. When the question moves from "Are you in favor of school choice?" to "What is school choice?" uniformity and agreement disappear. Some view choice as a highly laissez-faire proposal—a true education marketplace. Others envision choice as a strictly controlled policy that has its place but should be placed under tight government control.

Some uniformity returns when the question focuses on the likely outcomes of a choice program. The answers only partly agree with the theoretical positives promoted by choice programs. Most agree that, regardless of its form, choice will benefit some. It is also likely to harm, or at least isolate, others—the "bad" students whom nobody wants as classmates. Advocates argue that with proper governmental controls, school choice will not promote racial segregation. The white and black tenth graders interviewed flatly disagree. Given a choice, the majority of them said the racial composition of a school would play a large role in their enrollment decisions. The question of religion also proves to be a divisive element only thinly covered by the positive connotation of the choice label. Most public school students with experience in parochial schools saw little need to include them in choice programs. Parochial school students and officials at least partially framed school choice as a freedom-of-religion issue.

Adding up the experiences of individual students, teachers, and parents to get a clear picture of what is wrong with schools and how they can be fixed is difficult. This lack of agreement justifies a healthy dose of skepticism in viewing any plan or program that claims to have identified *the* problem of American education and to have concocted a universal prescription to solve it. Sick people who read labels do not drink snake oil, and there as yet has been no label printed about school choice. This book is designed to provide some of the missing fine print on the school choice prescription bottle.

Notes

1. The story of the list presented here is based on O'Neill's 1994 essay, and the contents of the list are those quoted by O'Neill. As O'Neill documents,

however, the list is often changed, rearranged, or updated. Differing versions have been quoted as authoritative, although all apparently have the same source.

2. Milwaukee Public Schools also operate a variety of experimental programs within the school system. In general students may attend the school of their choice within the district, subject to openings and racial distributions. The system is built around specialty magnet schools that range from academic preparation to schools for the arts and language and cultural immersion schools. Wisconsin also operates a school choice experimental program involving private, nonsectarian schools (see Witte 1991; Witte et al. 1992). Several private foundations have also underwritten a school choice program by providing aid to parents who send their children to private schools. This program permits participation by religious schools.

3. Because of concerns expressed by parents and various school administrations, none of the students are being fully identified. Further details on these interviews are available from the authors.

4. These statistics are reported in the "1992–93 Report Card Summary," issued by the MPS Department of Public Affairs.

5. Rufus King achieved a great deal of prominence in 1994 when it won the state academic decathlon and subsequently placed in the top ten nationally. The state title had routinely been won by suburban schools in previous years.

6. There is one other difference: Bruce Guadalupe is a bilingual school. Other public schools in the Milwaukee area have bilingual programs including some immersion programs, but such arrangements tend to be the exception rather than the rule.

———— Two ————

Problems, Solutions, and Choices

For more than a decade, numerous reports have claimed that the nation's education system is failing. As evidence, critics have pointed to falling achievement test scores, high dropout rates, and comparative studies showing American students to be academically behind their counterparts in other nations.[1] That inferior schools threaten the nation's economic future and its status as a global leader in science and technology has become almost an article of faith.

So bleak is the prognosis for education that there are increasing calls for radical reform—not for action from the existing system, but for its elimination. The education system is so bad, the problems so intractable, some critics say it must be replaced entirely. In the vanguard of this effort to replace the status quo is the vaguely defined but increasingly popular notion of school choice.[2] School choice calls for eliminating the governing structures of schools in favor of decentralization and deregulation. Students and parents would be given vouchers to spend at a school of their choice. Choice advocates argue that market economics can cure America's ailing schools. Competition will provide the incentive to improve educational quality, and the result will be an overall improvement in public education. Whether the problem is falling achievement test scores or high dropout rates, influential research such as that done by John Chubb and Terry Moe (1988, 1990) argues that choice can provide the solution.

The "solution," however, may not have a problem to cure. Despite the gloomy statistics and the firm public perception of a system in crisis, a convincing argument can be mounted that America's schools are not only performing well but are improving. Because the effects of dismantling the existing system and replacing it with one based on choice may have potentially devastating effects on quality and equity, we should be sure that we have a problem, and that we know exactly what that problem is, before adopting radical reform proposals.

Are America's schools really as bad as they seem? Will a choice-based education system work better? This research offers an explanation of why the answer to both questions is no.

Problems or Perceptions?

The alarm raised over the nation's educational slide is seemingly justified. From 1974 to 1990 mean SAT scores slipped from a national average of 924 to 900 (see Table 2.1). Internationally, the statistics are equally depressing. Thirteen-year-old U.S. students were last in a seven-nation 1991 comparison of science and math achievement.[3] The most famous analysis of America's schools during the past decade was without dramatization entitled *A Nation at Risk* (National Commission on Excellence in Education 1983). Other reports echoed the concerns of critics of the education system (Twentieth Century Fund 1983; Task Force on Education for Economic Growth 1983). John Chubb and Terry Moe (1990, 1) can offer a lengthy list of empirical studies to back their claim that "America's children are not learning enough, they are not learning the right things, and, most debilitating of all, they are not learning how to learn."

A closer examination of the "evidence," however, reveals that the statistical portrait of an education system in crisis may be misleading. Falling Scholastic Aptitude Test (SAT) scores are the most commonly offered proof of an education system in crisis (Henig 1994, 27). Yet the primary reason for SAT declines is not diminishing quality of education but changes in demographics. Since the mid-1970s, the pool of students taking the SAT has changed dramatically. There are fewer students taking the SAT who rank in the top 20 percent of their high school class than there were fifteen years ago. To an increasing number of test takers, English is a second language. More minorities—who tend to score lower on achievement tests—now take the SAT (see Table 2.2). While minorities make up a larger percentage of test takers, all minority subgroups have improved their SAT scores in the past fifteen years, while scores for whites have remained stable (see Table 2.3). If 1990 SAT scores are weighted to reflect the demographic makeup of the 1975 pool of test takers, scores actually improved by 30 points in fifteen years (Sandia National Laboratories 1993, 267–70).

Table 2.1

Mean SAT Scores, 1974–90

School year	Verbal	Math	Total
1974–75	444	480	924
1975–76	431	472	903
1977–78	429	468	897
1978–79	427	467	894
1979–80	424	466	890
1980–81	424	466	890
1981–82	426	467	893
1982–83	425	468	893
1983–84	426	471	897
1984–85	431	475	906
1986–87	430	476	906
1987–88	428	476	904
1988–89	427	476	903
1989–90	424	476	900

Source: Digest of Education Statistics for the years cited.

Table 2.2

Ethnic Composition of SAT Test Takers, 1975–90

Year	Percentage of test takers		
	White	Black	Other
1975	86.0	7.9	6.1
1977	83.9	8.8	7.3
1978	83.0	9.0	8.0
1979	82.9	8.9	8.2
1980	82.1	9.1	8.8
1981	81.9	9.0	9.1
1982	81.7	8.9	9.4
1983	81.1	8.8	10.1
1984	80.3	9.1	10.6
1985	82.1	9.1	8.8
1987	78.2	8.7	13.1
1988	77.0	9.2	13.8
1989	74.7	9.6	15.7
1990	73.0	10.0	17.0

Source: U.S. Statistical Abstract for the years cited.
Note: Figures for 1976 and 1986 are unavailable.

Table 2.3

Mean SAT Scores by Ethnicity, 1975–90

School year	White Verbal	Math	Black Verbal	Math	Mexican American Verbal	Math
1975–76	451	493	332	354	371	410
1977–78	446	485	332	354	370	402
1978–79	444	483	330	358	370	410
1979–80	442	482	330	360	372	413
1980–81	442	483	332	362	373	415
1981–82	444	483	341	366	377	416
1982–83	443	484	339	369	375	417
1983–84	445	487	342	373	376	420
1984–85	449	490	346	376	382	426
1986–87	447	489	351	377	379	424
1987–88	445	490	353	384	382	428
1988–89	446	491	351	386	381	430
1989–90	442	491	352	385	380	429

Source: U.S. Statistical Abstract for the years cited.

Even without such statistical manipulations, SAT scores have remained stable since the mid-1970s (Table 2.3).

In the 1990s a much more socioeconomically diverse group of test takers is improving even in the misleading columns of raw scores. In 1993 the mean SAT scores for all students improved significantly for the second year in a row, and the improvements were attributed to stricter academic requirements mandated by states (De Witt 1993). Similarly, both graduation and dropout rates also improved between 1975 and 1990 (Sandia National Laboratories 1993, 261–65).

While work such as Kozol's (1991) portrays a system that has failed and all but abandoned the inner city, evidence suggests that even the most beleaguered schools are helping students. The Council of the Great City Schools (1992, xiv), representing the nation's forty largest urban school districts, reports that "there is good evidence to show that urban schools are doing unusually well in the areas of childhood programming, advanced course placements, graduates' pursuit of four year colleges and universities, and in-school drug and alcohol abuse."

These successes have been achieved in an era of serious social problems ranging from the collapse of the inner-city family to increases in teen violence, and at a time when people demand that schools teach students how to deal with an ever more sophisticated and technological world. The constraints on the system are considerable, yet using the same measures touted as evidence of decline, America's schools are improving. On an average day, the public school system quite successfully tends to the education needs of more than 42 million students. Clearly, from a national perspective, the problem with American education has been exaggerated.

Serious problems do exist, but even if the sickness in American education has been overstated, the attraction of the cure represented by choice is unlikely to fade. Advocates of choice such as Chubb and Moe can argue that whatever the problems, real or imagined, they will only get worse. The reason is simple: the system is designed to fail. Although on closer examination the statistics may not fully support the critical diagnoses, enough symptoms exist to show the problems are real. Choice advocates claim to have identified the cause of virtually all education maladies: the institutional structures that control America's schools. This system has been incubating the sickness in education for the better part of a century, and choice is being offered as the cure.

The identification of institutions as *the* problem with education is rooted in the analysis of how public schools arrived at their current organizational makeup. The American educational system at the beginning of the century was very different from what we accept today as the status quo, and public choice advocates trace the current educational woes to the reforms of the past century. In the early part of the twentieth century private schools played a much greater role in education, accounting for 17.6 percent of total enrollment in 1900, roughly double that of today (U.S. Department of Education 1988). There was little centralization of power within the educational system, and consequently a great deal of local autonomy (Peterson 1985).

Much of this changed with the wave of reform heralded by the Progressive era. Education was increasingly placed in the hands of a centralized bureaucracy, which in turn was controlled by democratic institutions.[4] This occurred at the local level, where the superintendent and the school board were the bureaucratic and democratic institutions of interest, and at the state level, where a state superintendent of schools or similar office and the legislature performed parallel functions. The result was more uniformity in the way schools were operated, the "one best system."[5] As described by Chubb and Moe (1990, 4) the one best system "was bureaucratic and professional, designed to ensure, so the story goes, that education would be taken out of politics and placed in the hands of impartial experts devoted to the public interest." Centralization, however, was limited. Although the federal government has become more involved over the past several decades, historically it has had little interest in, and even less control over, primary and secondary education. Some states exert substantial control over education, but other states play only a marginal role.

The extent of bureaucratization and centralization is a matter of controversy. Some see the public school system as a monopoly, ruthlessly assembled by power-maximizing education professionals at the expense of local control over schools (Peterson 1990). Others reject this view, arguing that individual actors within the system retain a great deal of autonomy and that much of this is concentrated at the local level (Witte 1990; Tyack 1990; Ziegler 1974).

Those such as Peterson, who argue that public education is monopolistic, also tend to argue that as a monopoly with control over supply, the current system has little incentive to change. Certainly this argument is pursued to its logical extreme by Chubb and Moe (1990), who argue that institutions controlling the system are incapable of reforms to solve the nation's pressing educational problems because they *are* the problem. While willing to make changes, such institutions will not take actions detrimental to their primary clientele—the education bureaucracy and the democratic institutions that control them. Schools, in the view of those who argue that education is a monopoly, are more interested in protecting turf than pursuing meaningful and effective education reform.[6]

While the statistics may be open to question, for choice supporters the institutional cause of the problems in education is not. Because unresponsive institutions are the problem, the obvious solution is to get rid of them, replacing them with decentralized, autonomous schools that must serve the demands of parents and students rather than those of bureaucrats and teachers' unions.

Previous Research and the Beginnings of Choice

While those in favor of decentralization see the roots of educational decline in institutional structures—that is, in the schools themselves— other research argues that schools have virtually no impact on student performance. If institutions are impotent to affect educational quality, then they can hardly be blamed for educational decline. For many years, the major findings presented by social science indicated that the most influential factors affecting school performance were beyond the control of educational institutions and policy. Such dismal conclusions were trotted out to the educational community by social scientists at least dating back to 1966, the year of the famous Coleman Report. This work used the now-familiar education function model—where education outputs are modeled as functions of various inputs—and found school inputs have relatively little impact on student performance.

Although controversial, basic findings of the Coleman Report were consistently corroborated. For years, virtually all research done in this area found traditional remedies for improving school performance to be ineffective (for authoritative reviews of this literature see Hanushek 1981, 1986; Chubb and Moe 1990; Bryk, Lee, and Smith 1990; Henig 1994). Instead, cognitive abilities and family background (Coleman et al. 1966, Jencks et al. 1972) and socioeconomic considerations (Morgan and Watson 1987; Wahlberg and Rasher 1979; Bridge, Judd, and Moock 1979) have repeatedly been shown to be the major determinants of student performance. Exceptions to these general findings exist (e.g., Sharkansky 1967; Gailbraith 1984; Ferguson 1991); but if any consensus emerged from the social science research on student performance following the path-breaking work done by Coleman and his colleagues, it was this: family background matters; money and the policies it supports do not.[7]

If this convincing stream of research is correct, then the future of American education appears gloomy indeed, and choice seems a pointless reform because the problem is not the schools but the students who attend them. In many of the nation's most troubled schools, poverty, teenage pregnancy, fractured families, crime, and a host of other social problems are woven into the fabric of daily life for most students (Kozol 1991). Because educational policy can at best have a limited impact on such broad social crises, it is hard to fathom how educational policymakers can realistically hope to improve student performance given the limited resources at their disposal. Simply put, this literature seems to indicate that when it comes to student performance, the factors that appear to count the most are beyond the control and influence of educational policymakers, regardless of where they stand on the centralization versus decentralization debate.

Prior Reforms

Antidotes for the faltering educational system have never been in short supply, and school choice is just the latest to attract the attention of policymakers. Most of the reports sparking the reforms of the 1980s included a list of policy suggestions; many were adopted. A proportion of these, however, were policy options social science had already identified as minimally effective. Increased teacher salaries, for example, was a reform often championed within the education community as a step toward improving performance. The pressure for increased salaries continued throughout the 1980s and wages in the educational field rose accordingly.[8] The argument that better wages attract better teachers and better teachers produce better students has consistently found very little empirical confirmation (Hanushek 1981).

Still, many of these reforms went beyond the usual list of money-related variables social science research has often made the primary focus of its research. Widespread teacher certification tests became the norm in the 1980s, years of mandatory attendance were increased, academic standards were stiffened, and numerous other education-related policies were pursued in an attempt to revamp student performance.[9]

Many of the policy reforms of the 1980s grew out of the voluminous "effective schools" research that critically reassessed the work of Coleman and others and concluded that schools can make a difference (for good reviews of this literature, see Purkey and Smith 1983; Corcoran 1985; Rosenholtz 1985). This literature essentially zeroed in on a widely criticized flaw in the model employed by the Coleman Report and much of the subsequent corroborating research. The inputs of the Coleman model were for the most part funding related or consisted of quantifiable variables such as number of books in a school library. These inputs were seen as dubious indicators of the ability of schools to affect student performance. Factors such as effective organization and individual school leadership were completely ignored. In reexamining the conclusions drawn by the Coleman research, the effective schools literature concluded that schools can make a difference. And if schools can make a difference, it is simply a matter of identifying those variables that positively affect student performance. Once identified, these characteristics can be widely copied with a resulting universal boost in student performance. This is essentially what policymakers attempted to do during the 1980s.[10]

Despite an improvement in dropout rates and an arrest in the decline of standardized test scores, the widespread perception remains that the reforms failed and that the educational system continues to decline. Work such as Kozol's (1991) gives alarming support to such a perception, even though a comprehensive analysis of the effects of these reforms has yet to be undertaken. These perceived failures have bolstered the arguments of the decentralists, and the increasing dissatisfaction with the status quo has fueled the growing political and popular support for school choice. Schools do make a difference, they contend, and judging from their performance, that difference is not always positive.

School choice advocates argue that the policy mimicry emerging from the effective schools literature is doomed to failure. What works for one school will not necessarily work for all schools. Schools should be free to promote reforms and innovations that meet the unique demands of their own clientele without being forced into imitating solutions that, although successful elsewhere, may have little connection to local need. While identifying organizational features of schools that boost student performance, the effective schools literature has done little to explain how such characteristics can be transferred (Chubb and Moe 1990, 17). Chubb and Moe's argument in favor of "pure" school choice presents a provocative argument, not for reforming the existing educational system, but for replacing it entirely. Their work has provided a firm foundation for the growth of the school choice movement.

School Choice

Despite its relatively recent arrival as a popular and realistic policy option, school choice has a long history. Milton Friedman, an economist, proposed a well-developed school voucher system more than three decades ago, and since then choice has waxed and waned in the education arena (see Henig 1994, 57–77). Its emergence in the 1980s from decades of indifference has been attributed to the growing popularity of a broad privatization movement pushed by Republican presidential administrations and its skillful positioning as an individual-based antidote to the education crisis (Henig 1994, 78–96).

As political scientist Jeffrey Henig has argued, however, the recent reincarnation of choice has been less as a concrete policy proposal and more as an intuitively appealing market metaphor. The label of choice has a strong positive connotation. Many people seem to support the notion of choice without any real idea of what a school choice program will entail. When the shift from abstraction to reality is made, choice loses much of its luster (Henig 1994, 174–95).

There are many versions of school choice. Voucher plans, choice limited to public schools, programs that include private schools, intradistrict choice, interdistrict choice, voluntary and involuntary open enrollment polices. While a universally appealing metaphor, there is virtually no agreement on what policy translation the school choice metaphor should take.

School choice, however, does have at least one candidate for a unifying theory that steps beyond the metaphor and offers concrete answers. In their book *Politics, Markets and America's Schools* (1990), Chubb and Moe lay out a well-developed theoretical model of school choice. This work has provided much of the intellectual support for the growing choice movement. As a result of its role as *the* theoretical center of school choice, it is Chubb and Moe's work that we take as our model of school choice and their theory that we propose to test.

As argued by Chubb and Moe, effective organization holds the key to improved student performance, and school choice offers the best promise of effectively organized schools. The notion that effective organization is the key to improved educational performance has been gathering force since social science research began exploring the differences between public and private schools. Some research has concluded that private schools do a better job of educating students than public schools (Coleman and Hoffer 1987; Coleman, Hoffer, and Kilgore 1982). Public choice analysts have concluded the reason for this lies in the organizational differences between the public and private sector. Chubb and Moe (1988, 1069) argue that control by democratic institutions promotes ineffective organization and limits autonomy, essentially constraining the ability of schools to respond appropriately to the educational demands of their clientele. Schools are forced to serve their democratic masters, not parents and students. Because education is a monopoly, students have no realistic option to seek a better school and schools have no incentives to change. The effective schools literature also linked academic performance to certain organizational characteristics, lending greater empirical support to the public choice claims that organization is of paramount importance in affecting school performance.[11]

School choice supporters see private schools as less constrained by political actors than public schools, and it is this autonomy that is the key to their success. In the public system legislatures and school boards set goals and enforce compliance through a bureaucratic hierarchy. Bureaucracies require forms, procedures, and auditing mechanisms. The requirements limit the actions schools make take. Schools are consequently more responsive to outside political constituencies than to their own students. As put bluntly by Chubb and Moe (1990, 564), ". . . private schools possess these desirable organizational characteristics to a far greater extent than public schools do." The reason for this advantage is that private schools are governed by the market instead of by democratic institutions and hierarchical bureaucracies. If public schools were freed from democratic control and bureaucratic constraints, and instead regulated by the market, they could repeat the success of private schools.

Anthony Downs (1966, 5) argues that bureaucracy is created "in order to carry out a specific function." Bureaucracy acts as a management mechanism for democratic institutions; it is used as an instrument for policy implementation, formulation, and enforcement. Theoretically, at least, public bureaucracies take their marching orders from democratic institutions, and it is this organizational structure that Chubb and Moe argue is fundamental to the problems with the educational system. Such institutions are responsive to a number of groups with a vested interest in educational policies: teachers' unions, business groups, education bureaucrats. Parents and students are but one of these constituencies. As a group, they tend to be less organized and have a harder time making the system responsive to their demands than, say, a teachers' union. Control by democratic institutions has meant the system is responsive to constituents rather than consumers (Chubb and Moe 1990, 30–35). In essence, the school system has no incentive to respond to parental and student demands for better educational quality.

As already discussed, the social science literature supports two perspectives on the organization of American public schools. One holds public schools to be centralized, bureaucratic, and hierarchically subordinate to other administrative agencies and democratic institutions (Peterson 1990; Chubb and Moe 1990). In contrast to this view are empirical descriptions of a decentralized system with a good deal of local autonomy and independence among relevant actors (Witte 1990). School choice advocates—that is, those who decry the unresponsiveness of institutions in their "institutional theory"—see the former and want the latter. The organizational dichotomy is directly related to the prescriptive conclusions drawn on improving student performance. School choice supporters see much of the problem rooted in the organizational and institutional flaws of the existing system. Chubb and Moe view the flaws as endemic and advocate decoupling education from democratic institutions and putting it under the control of the market.

Freeing individual schools from external political constituencies and a stifling bureaucratic hierarchy will allow them to respond to the educational concerns of students and parents. Following the basic economic law of supply and demand, parents and students will be attracted to schools that fulfill those educational needs. Dollars will be awarded to educational institutions on a per student basis, and those schools, public or private, doing the best job of meeting the demands of their potential "customer base" will be rewarded. Using the blunt instrument of money, the market will supply the incentive for educational improvement. The institutions that do not respond to the demands of the marketplace will be punished.

Although this may seem a persuasive argument, empirically testing the claims of school choice has proven to be difficult. Choice is not precisely defined, and comparable data are lacking. In general, however, the empirical studies on existing choice programs in the United States have not confirmed the promised benefits of a market-based solution to slipping educational quality (e.g., Witte 1991, 1992; Witte, Bailey, and Thorn 1992; Sosniak and Ethington 1992; but see also Fliegel and MacGuire 1993). Probably the most comprehensive studies of school choice done to date are those conducted by the U.S. Department of Education (1992b), the Carnegie Foundation (1992), and political scientist Jeffrey Henig (1994). None corroborates the promised benefits of choice. The Carnegie Foundation report in particular found that although choice does indeed provide important benefits in specific cases, overall its impact is mixed. Among other things, this study reported that choice's effect on academic improvement was far from uniform, that participation in the existing programs is extremely low, and that choice can be a tremendously expensive reform to implement and sustain (Carnegie Foundation 1992, 9–28). Where choice has been implemented and studied in other countries, the results have been mixed or disappointing (e.g., Adler, Petch, and Tweedie 1989; Bowe, Ball, and Gold 1992).

Despite the failure of the promised benefits of choice to appear, as a policy prescription choice continues gaining public and popular support. Thirteen states have adopted some form of choice legislation, many experimental programs are being conducted at the district or school level, and groups such as the National Governors' Association (1986, 12) have endorsed choice as a worthy policy goal. Ideology rather than systematic empirical investigation is often the material fueling the choice debate. As Eric Boyer has written, "there's an intensity, even a zealousness in the debate on school choice that smothers thoughtful discourse." In the absence of convincing empirical evidence for either side, the choice controversy continues to be a focal point of disagreement among scholars and within the popular press (e.g., Allen 1991; Bainbridge and Sundre 1991; Boswell 1990; Carr 1991; Gibson 1991; Judis 1991; Thernstrom 1991; Whealey 1991).

Regardless of the evidence or lack of it, as a policy option choice continues to gain adherents. After devoting more than a year to compiling their report on public choice, researchers at the Carnegie Foundation (1992, 9) found that "in states and districts where choice has been adopted, little effort has been made to record the process carefully or to document results. Anecdotes have been used to justify new initiatives. Sweeping legislation has been passed with little planning, and we were left with the clear impression that critical policy decisions are being made based more on faith than on fact."

Beyond the questionable performance payoffs is the unknown impact of public choice on equity. Universal access, backed by force of law since the desegregation litigation of the past three decades, has been a central goal of the American education system. Although desegregation efforts have been unable to halt discrimination against minorities (Meier, Stewart, and England 1989), and desegregation in some areas, particularly urban ones, may be a cruel fiction (Kozol 1991), universal access remains a goal of central importance to the education system. Anything that promotes increased school segregation is, for obvious reasons, believed to be counterproductive to the nation's educational goals.

Research such as that done by the Carnegie Foundation indicates that school choice holds the potential to construct a system that financially punishes weak educational institutions, thus exacerbating the already considerable problems of schools attempting to educate a socioeconomically disadvantaged, predominantly minority, portion of the nation's student population.[12] Given a choice between a well-funded school with a diverse curriculum in a safe suburb and a school consisting of a crumbling building in a crime-ridden inner city, few would take the latter over the former. In a public choice system the former would benefit financially by providing the better educational product and attracting more students. Expecting the entire clientele of the latter, however, to gravitate toward the suburbs is unrealistic. Transportation and information costs will play a large role in student placement in a school choice system, as will the simple dictates of building space.[13] What happens to those left behind? They will be trapped in inferior institutions providing inferior educations and will be deprived of the resources they so desperately need.

Nor do school choice advocates address some of the general problems of marketplaces that might not be acceptable in an educational setting. Markets punish companies that do not respond to the market with bankruptcy. People who have purchased goods from a firm that ceases to exist are simply left holding the bag (or the Edsel, as the case may be); they no longer have access to any service or warranties that were part of the sale price. Similar problems could occur in school choice programs. If a school closes because it fails to meet the demands of parents, what happens to students who were attending the school? Those students have lost the time they have invested in the school; they must immediately scramble to find another school that is willing to take them, perhaps even repeating a grade. This is not a hypothetical situation. In the experimental Milwaukee choice program, the Juanita Hill school closed its doors in the middle of the first year. Students attending Juanita Hill were subsequently dumped on the public school system.

School choice advocates also do not talk about another element of market system incentives. Not only do companies have an incentive to respond to market demands, but they also have the incentive to respond to this demand by using as few resources as possible so as to maximize profits. Some schools might promise more than they can deliver or seek to cut costs where the impact on performance is not readily available. Companies can succeed either with a superior product or with a superior marketing program. A program with many characteristics of school choice, the college student loan program, continually faces this problem. Many vocational schools make grand promises. When students become disillusioned and go elsewhere, the school can continue to prosper by enticing the next set of students. All markets have a dark side; only in a market highly lated by government organizations with knowledgeable consumers are such market problems minimized. Whether markets for education can avoid such problems has yet to be demonstrated.

Because the stakes are so high, empirically investigating whether choice will improve education overall or whether a competitive system will favor some at the expense of others is critical. Since Chubb and Moe provided the catalyst for the choice debate with their influential research, there has been much criticism, but little in the way of comprehensive empirical analysis. This research seeks to fill that gap.

Conclusion

School choice is a policy option being pursued with increasing vigor across the nation. Touted as a reform vehicle that will halt America's educational slide, it promises to improve educational quality by putting schools under the control of a free market. Empowered parents and students will select the school that best fits their educational needs, and the tax dollars spent to support a particular pupil's education will follow that individual to his or her chosen institution. Schools, freed from constraining exogenous constituencies, will compete as entrepreneurs, and the market will reward those who best fill the demands of their clientele. The end result will be improved educational quality and more satisfied parents and teachers.

Such is the promise. Empirical investigation of these claimed benefits, however, is slim. The multiple goals of this research are aimed at analyzing the as yet unanswered questions surrounding school choice. Are schools really as bad as they seem? Are the politics of education merely symbolic, and are reforms from the existing educational structure doomed to failure? Will school choice improve educational quality? If so, will it upset the already precarious balance of equity within the education system? If school choice does not work, what will?

In order to answer these questions we propose a systematic examination. First we examine the theoretical underpinnings of school choice as put forward by Chubb and Moe. From their institutional-based theory we develop a set of hypotheses on the expected relationships between education performance and the institutional characteristics of education systems. We then put these to the empirical acid test.

Notes

1. The perception that education in the United States lags behind other industrialized nations is not universally shared by social scientists. Some political scientists, especially those who study cross-national voting behavior, consider the United States "to have the most educated citizenry" (Powell 1986, 31). Such judgments are based on comparisons of graduation rates—more people complete high school in the United States than virtually anywhere else. Graduation rates, however, are dubious measures of educational attainment. In standardized math and science testing, U.S. students consistently rank at or near the bottom of comparative studies.

2. Evidence of this support is found in a number of state referendums, most recently in California, proposing a choice-based education system. While gaining enough support to be placed on the ballot, choice has yet to win a majority of a popular vote at the state level.

3. All figures taken from National Center for Education Statistics (1992c).

4. These reforms were pushed by business in the private sector. The resulting system also seems much *less* democratic than the system it replaced. The reformers took control of education away from politics and patronage and placed it in the hands of professionals who were more insulated from the electorate.

5. The "one best system" is a label popularized by David B. Tyack (1974) from his book of the same name.

6. This view of bureaucracy seems contradictory, that is, it portrays a bureaucracy both highly responsive to political forces and jealously protective of its turf. Many scholars have adopted one of these perspectives, but it is hard to incorporate both into a single philosophy.

7. Money, especially, has been shown repeatedly to be of limited effectiveness as a way to improve educational quality. Beyond the authoritative reviews of Hanushek (1981, 1986) is the fact that the United States scores lowest on international academic comparisons while spending the most on public education, both in terms of per pupil expenditures and GNP devoted to education. See National Center for Education Statistics (1992c, 52–53 and 133.)

8. Between 1980 and 1990 the average teacher salary in the United States grew approximately 20 percent, from $26,995 to $30,981 in constant (1989) dollars (U.S. Department of Education 1992a). Teacher salaries thus far outpaced inflation.

9. For a good overview of the education reforms enacted in the past decade, see the National Center for Education Statistics, *Overview and Inventory of State Requirements for School Coursework and Attendance* (1992b). The data Chubb and Moe use to give empirical support for their choice prescriptions were gathered before many of these reforms were enacted.

10. Even the effective schools literature offered no blanket support for the reforms of the 1980s. Instructional reforms, such as those aimed at maximizing student learning time, often ran counter to the conclusions drawn from this body of research (see Bryck, Lee, and Smith 1990, 163).

11. Although the effective schools literature contains much support for the school choice perspective, Chubb and Moe (1990, 14–18) ironically reject most of its findings.

12. The nation's forty-seven largest school districts constitute 13.1 percent of the total student population, but 37.1 percent of total African American enrollment, 31.8 percent of Hispanic enrollment, and 24.5 percent of those students classified as poor (Council of the Great City Schools 1992).

13. All three of these variables are prominently mentioned in reports done by Witte and the Carnegie Foundation.

————— Three —————

The Institutional Theory:
School Choice Revisited

Any attempt to conduct a comprehensive empirical test of whether a public choice system will work runs into an immediate problem—as yet there is no such system to test. While programs ranging from state to school level have been adopted, these programs share little uniformity in approach and even less in the area of comparable data collection (Henig 1994). Empirical studies so far have concentrated on individual choice programs or comparisons of limited numbers of public and choice or private schools.

In short, lack of data has thus far limited the scope of research. Certainly no empirical test worthy of the sweeping institutional theory Chubb and Moe have presented as a universal explanatory model of education has been undertaken. Instead, most research consists of isolated district or state successes used to bolster the arguments that the system works (e.g., Honig 1990–91), glowing descriptive pieces on pilot programs to demonstrate the "miracle" of choice (e.g., Fliegel and MacGuire 1993), or reviews of existing literature.

Manhattan's Community School District 4 in East Harlem, one of New York City's most impoverished neighborhoods, is probably the most widely used example of the benefits of enacting a school choice system (e.g., Chubb and Moe 1990, 212–15). After enacting a pioneering choice system in 1974, East Harlem was soon reporting dramatic improvements in test scores and its overall learning environment. In East Harlem the school district was decentralized into many autonomous "concept" schools. Schools in District 4 offer a veritable buffet of education to students. East Harlem's schools include the Academy of Environmental Sciences, the Isaac Newton School for Math and Science, and the Harbor Performing Arts School. Students are free to choose from these diverse offerings.[1]

Less publicized by choice advocates is the experience of the Richmond Unified School District of California. In 1989 the district "was recognized as a national model of successful public school choice" and was chosen by the U.S. Education Department as one of five locations for national conferences on choice. A few years later, Richmond's experiment in choice ended in disaster. After initial favorable publicity, the program failed to achieve any of its stated objectives. Choice failed to improve test scores, dropout rates, and absenteeism, or to promote desegregation. In addition, the financial burden of implementing the program drove the district into bankruptcy (Chriss, Nash, and Stern 1992).

Even choice's successes have been criticized. To underwrite the East Harlem project, on a per student basis it became the most expensive federally subsidized system in the nation (Carnegie Foundation 1992, 24). To achieve this level of support required the active involvement of certain sectors of the political system—up to and including President George Bush—that backed choice on ideological grounds. Thus critics can claim East Harlem is a success because of the intervention of the very democratic control system that choice seeks to eliminate. Given the ambiguous results, empirical studies on one or a handful of programs seem no more likely to end the debate on choice than the ideologically based arguments on choice.

Chubb and Moe have laid the groundwork for a comprehensive empirical test of school choice. Their institutional theory is presented as a universal explanatory model of how education works. The institutional perspective embodies the foundation of public choice. It also offers a rich source of testable hypotheses on the relationships between institutional and organizational structure and educational performance. Comparable data to test these relationships are available across school districts and states.

Putting the institutional theory to the empirical test is, in effect, a test of whether the school choice movement has correctly identified what is wrong with education. If the institutional theory can be confirmed in a comprehensive empirical fashion, it will show that the public choice argument has correctly unveiled *the* problem in education. This identification is the basis for why a choice system will work, and empirical support for the institutional theory will confirm the causal dynamics driving the choice argument. If confirmation is not forthcoming, then the theoretical supports begin to crumble; and only ideology remains to shore up the public choice argument. The institutional theory thus provides a basis for a comprehensive empirical test of school choice.

Chubb and Moe's institutional theory outlines the causal links between institutional structure and performance, and posits relationships that can be empirically tested. Although widely criticized (e.g., Riley 1990; Tweedie 1990; Witte 1992; Bryk and Lee 1992), this institutional theory seems to be a particularly useful tool for examining the utility of school choice.

Despite its perceived flaws, Chubb and Moe's institutional theory has performed a service to the debate on education. It is one of the few existing attempts at universal explanation in education, as opposed to piecemeal examinations of lists of variables (Chubb and Moe 1990, 565). The theory is in large part responsible for shifting the focus of the debate on educational performance from what goes on in schools to the institutions that control them (Best 1993). An examination of the role of these institutions, as Chubb and Moe argue, was certainly overdue.

In approaching the question of educational performance from the perspective of schools' institutional environments, Chubb and Moe present the most well developed argument on behalf of public choice. Although poorly received in some quarters, no serious rival to the institutional theory in terms of universal explanation has emerged. While doubters have picked at pieces of the institutional theory, no real attempt has been made to develop a comprehensive empirical test.

This lack of empirical attention is surprising. The institutional theory holds the promise of providing some hard answers to the questions about the merits of school choice. Whether the institutional theory is valid is an empirical proposition. What our research will do is take the institutional perspective used as a theoretical guide by Chubb and Moe, develop hypotheses from it, and test them empirically. Outlining in detail the institutional theory, its perceived flaws, and testable hypotheses that can resolve arguments over its validity is therefore important.

Assumptions

In laying out their institutional theory, Chubb and Moe make several a priori assumptions. First and foremost, they assume a large pool of unsatisfied demand for an educational product superior to that offered in public schools. Although such an assumption seems to be widely shared by politicians and policymakers, skeptics claim there is little empirical evidence to support it.

Instead, geography seems to be the dominant factor in choosing a school. For example, after Minnesota enacted its statewide open-enrollment policy, students did not suddenly migrate from "bad" schools to "good" schools. In fact, in 1991–92, five years after its enactment, only 13,000 of the state's 749,000 students—less than 2 percent—took advantage of the choice option open to them and switched schools (Carnegie Foundation 1992, 105).[2]

The demand assumption is based on a view of parents and students as rational actors. Within the education marketplace these consumers will seek to maximize benefits and minimize costs. Borrowed from economics, the idea of the rational person has been used by the social sciences with varying degrees of success. The benefits of a good education, however, seem to make students and parents good candidates for rational behavior. Surely, school choice advocates argue, to parents it is worth the cost of gathering information on comparable schools if it benefits the child. Getting information to parents, however, has proven to be one of the major hurdles faced by existing choice programs. Outreach efforts are an expensive burden (Chriss, Nash, and Stern 1992; Carnegie Foundation 1992, 23). Transportation costs involved in getting a student to another school and the emotional trauma of leaving one school for another may also complicate the view of simple demand for quality education as the driving force within an educational marketplace.

Placing the unresolved debate over the utility of rational actor models aside, the demand assumption made by Chubb and Moe is an empirical question. If there is a demand for quality education and there is a choice between schools, there should be a movement toward the "better" schools. If such a movement fails to materialize, the a priori assumption of demand is wrong.

Another a priori assumption made by Chubb and Moe is uniformity among the institutions that govern public education. They essentially adopt the viewpoint of public education portrayed by researchers such as Peterson (1990). Because they assume institutions are uniform within public education, Chubb and Moe (1990, 27) compare public and private schools to show differences in institutional environments. This assumption also seems questionable. Based on the public-private comparison, Chubb and Moe argue that performance variation is caused solely by institutional differences. Yet performance among public schools varies widely. What is the source of such variation if it is not institutional? Why do some states consistently report higher achievement test scores than others? Why do some public high schools produce academic stars and others do not? If there "is no significant variation in institutions on which to base an enlightening analysis" among public schools, why are some doing better than others?

Such variation, of course, could come from outside demographic factors (i.e., exogenous variables), but the institutional theory treats schools' environmental and organizational characteristics as endogenous. Chubb and Moe (1990, 20) argue that school organization reflects the institutional setting, but they place little credence in interactions with a broader environment. "We are not comfortable with a level of abstraction that encourages macroscopic—and usually mysterious—talk about schools and their environments." This seems to cut off the possibility of external environmental pressures as an explanation for performance variation and thus undercuts their whole argument on private schools.

Chubb and Moe have never answered the question on public school variation to the satisfaction of their critics (e.g., Tweedie 1990, 550). Again, this variation and its causes are an empirical proposition. If differing characteristics of public education institutions can be identified and demonstrated to affect performance across systems, then Chubb and Moe's assumption is wrong. If the external environment is influencing public school variation, then the internal focus of the institutional theory is flawed.

Democratic Control

The institutional theory is strongly antidemocratic. It sees democratic control as the tail that wags the education dog. Democratic control means that centralized decision-making bodies force their will on the recipients of education services. These recipients have little say in formulating the education product and, lacking choice, have to accept what is offered. By its very nature, democratic control is not designed to meet the needs or demands of parents or students (Chubb and Moe 1990, 32).

As described by Chubb and Moe, the authority to make decisions in a democracy is up for grabs. Parents and students can participate, but they have no assurance of winning, and "in the end, they have to take what society gives them." Parents and students make up but a small part of the democratic constituency, and on any given education issue other constituencies—ranging from teachers' unions to ideological special interests—may win the competitive democratic battle.[3] The winners of this struggle can enforce their values on the losers through the mechanism of hierarchical bureaucracy. The problem is not that the concerns of parents and students are ignored but that rival concerns have an equal right to compete for the public decision-making authority.

Even if students and parents were as effectively organized as the unions, professional groups, and other constituencies that successfully compete in the democratic arena, Chubb and Moe (1990, 32) say their concerns would not be satisfactorily addressed. Under democratic control, schools are "the agencies of society as a whole, and everyone has a right to participate in their governance." The democratic machinery takes the compromise-laden values of society and forces them on schools whether or not parents and students like the results. There is no incentive to respond to demands for higher educational quality from parents and students because the system is simply not designed to do that.

The institutional theory posits that the preferable way to regulate education is through the market. This is accomplished by eliminating democratic control and decentralizing authority to the individual school. Instead of responding to political institutions, schools will respond to the consumers of their services. Instead of democratic bodies deciding budgets and values, let dollars follow students and allow schools to compete for their patronage. Schools that best meet the demands for quality education will prosper, and those that fail will be eliminated.

The case against democratic control and for the market can be faulted on several points. These include questions of equity and accountability and assumptions on the role of education within society. To take the last point first, the argument in favor of markets assumes the primary function of public schools should be to meet the needs of the individual student. While not denying that this is an important function for public schools, society as a whole has a major stake in the system that educates its citizens. Education is a process that socializes children in the values of the nation; the importance of this function leads to several questions. Should tax dollars support schools that promote a particular ideology? Should religion be taught in schools? Is segregation allowable? Society beyond parents and students is affected by the answers to such questions and has a right to enter the debate (Honig 1990–91).

Society also has a huge stake in quality education. Economic survival—if we are to believe education critics—depends on it. If the bureaucratic machinery is so efficient at imposing the will of broader society on schools, then democratic control is logically a good choice to fulfill society's need for improved education. The institutional theory says the existing system is incapable of changing to improve education because it is not equipped to meet the demands of the individual. Again, using the same arguments encapsulated by the institutional theory, the current system seems admirably suited to impose the demands of society. If we are to believe the opinion polls brandished by education critics, society is demanding a better educational product. To achieve this desired societal end, democratic control is the obvious choice. This is, perhaps, a pedantic point.[4] Nonetheless, it is one school choice advocates often choose to ignore.

Democratic control also provides a method of accountability that is absent from the market. The institutional theory vests this responsibility in parents and students. This may be somewhat unrealistic. Parents or students may not have the resources to accomplish tasks such as audits on a regular basis. Without uniform reporting requirements enforced and collected by bureaucracy, schools will be free to release data on test scores, attendance, and graduation rates when and how they see fit. Parents may have difficulty in holding schools accountable if the schools control the information needed to judge performance and make comparisons. Indeed, one of the complaints that has consistently surfaced in studies on experimental choice programs is the need for accountability beyond that exercised by parents (e.g., Witte, Bailey, and Thorn 1992, 25).

Perhaps the most severe criticism leveled against the institutional theory is that market control will lead to increased trends in de facto segregation, hurting minorities and the poor (Honig 1990–91; U.S. House of Representatives Subcommittee on Elementary, Secondary, and Vocational Education 1990). Chubb and Moe counter by saying minorities will benefit from choice because they will be free to leave schools that provide a second-rate education. This is seen as potentially of great benefit to minority students trapped in impoverished inner-city schools. To expect entire urban schools to be vacated as students migrate to better facilities in the suburbs, however, is unrealistic. If nothing else, simple limits in building capacities and the massive transportation costs will mean some students undoubtedly will be left behind.

The institutional theory provides a number of testable hypotheses important to the debate over market versus democratic control of education. The theory predicts democratic control is bad because it limits a school's ability to respond to the demands of its primary clientele. Democratic control, therefore, is argued to be a causal factor in poor educational performance. As viewed by school choice advocates, the political institutions that control public education are uniform, hierarchical bureaucratic structures that have little chance of improving educational performance because they respond to the compromises of democratic politics, not the demands and needs of students. The policies of these institutions, therefore, are unlikely to improve educational performance significantly. The incentive to improve educational performance can be provided only by competition. Schools in a market environment will have to respond to demands for quality to survive. Competition, therefore, should increase education performance.

These propositions—that democratic control causes poor educational performance and that competition can improve it while existing institutions cannot—lie at the heart of the institutional theory. Together they constitute the logic driving the school choice movement. They, too, are empirical questions.

Bureaucracy

The institutional theory is somewhat ambivalent about bureaucracy. Chubb and Moe (1990, 45–47) make no secret that they see bureaucracy as bad for education, but they are reluctant to blame the bureaucrats. Although bureaucracy is portrayed as a negative influence on education, Chubb and Moe do not, as some opponents of central control do, attribute bureaucratic expansion to self-maximizing bureaucrats. Instead, they believe education was bureaucratized by politicians and interest groups in order to reduce "the discretion of schools and their personnel to ensure that America's children would be 'properly' educated, socialized, and disciplined" (Chubb and Moe 1990, 46). If democratic control is the cause of the education system's sickness, bureaucracy is seen as its most obvious symptom.[5]

Chubb and Moe recognize other sources of bureaucracy besides democratic control. Noting that school bureaucracies vary in size, they attribute these differences to the environments in which schools operate. Pressures to bureaucratize spring from problem-filled environments—where society encounters a problem, democracy tends to create a program and a bureaucracy to address it.[6] So, "schools with homogeneous, problem-free environments should tend to be the least bureaucratic, while schools with highly heterogeneous, problem-filled environments should tend to be the most bureaucratic" (Chubb and Moe 1990, 64).

Besides violating the institutional theory's initial focus on endogenous variables, this part of Chubb and Moe's institutional theory seems to come close to tautology. Bureaucracy is bad for schools, but bureaucracy is most likely to appear in schools with poor performance records resulting in part from environmental problems such as poverty, violence, and drugs. Is bureaucracy fulfilling needs—that is, meeting demands by society for a response to specific problems—or is it depressing performance by limiting autonomy and preventing schools from meeting the demands of their clientele? Chubb, Moe, and the institutional theory seem to side with the latter. But this sets up a self-fulfilling prophecy. Bureaucracy produces poorly performing schools; and poorly performing schools, because of the problems they face, produce bureaucracy.

Compounding the confusion of the role of bureaucracy in the institutional theory is that bureaucracy is never adequately defined. A well-developed literature points to bureaucracy as a complex multidimensional concept (e.g., Downs 1966). Chubb and Moe define bureaucracy somewhat sketchily as an organization that is hierarchical, rulebound, and formalistic, a description that could just as well be applied to IBM as to a school district central office. But this definition is useful because it fits with a common normative perception of why bureaucracy is bad: it ties down the potential of schools with mountains of red tape. Red tape is a common theme of choice advocates. Writing on the much-heralded East Harlem choice program, Seymore Fliegel and James MacGuire (1993, 25) declare that "centralized educational bureaucracies tend not to be concerned with higher motives (among faculty or students), seeking instead to satisfy and reassure their various constituencies—parents, unions, the press and so on—without exposing the system to failure and ridicule." While all choice advocates agree that bureaucracy is bad and less bureaucracy is better, exactly what bureaucracy is, is never made clear. Many choice supporters, including Chubb and Moe, seem to focus on the number of bureaucrats as evidence of too much bureaucracy (Fliegel and MacGuire 1993, 26–27).

Despite the murky definition and somewhat circular argument Chubb and Moe present on bureaucracy, the institutional theory is sufficiently robust to draw out a couple of testable hypotheses. First, bureaucracy—whatever it is—should be associated with poor school performance because, as the enforcer for democracy, it limits school autonomy. Second, a counterhypothesis is hinted: bureaucracy is a function of need produced by pressures from a school's external environment. The first hypothesis better fits the public choice model, which treats bureaucracy as a link between democratic control and a poor education system. The second hypothesis runs contrary to the public choice model, even though it was drawn from the institutional theory, which supports it. If bureaucracy is a function of need, then the exogenous socioeconomic environments of schools create bureaucracy, not the endogenous effects of the political institutions that control the system.

Goals and Unit of Analysis

The examination of Chubb and Moe's institutional theory of education provides the framework for an investigation into school choice claims. A list of empirical propositions drawn from the institutional theory and the counterhypotheses suggested by Chubb and Moe's critics is presented in Table 3.1. Together these represent a systematic test of the institutional theory and the school choice model it supports. Executing these tests will provide an empirical basis to judge the veracity of school choice as an education reform.

The empirical propositions provide an important guide to research, but they do not answer the question of what is to be studied. The choice of unit of analysis is a crucial factor in examining school choice. Chubb and Moe (1990, 21–22), for example, took the individual student as the unit of analysis, saying their perspective was people oriented: "It is about students, parents, teachers, principals, school board members, superintendents, politicians, interest group leaders, and others who have important roles to play in education." This is a logical progression from their focus on the view that the education system should serve the needs of the individual.

Table 3.1

Empirical Propositions Drawn from the Institutional Theory

Hypothesis	Counterhypothesis
1. The primary demand made by parents and students on schools is for quality education, and given the opportunity, they will seek to satisfy that demand.	1. Quality education is only one of several competing demands parents and students place on schools. Others include questions of race, geography, and religion.
2. Democratic control suppresses education performance by limiting autonomy and effective organization.	2. Democratic control is an appropriate mechanism to run education and does not suppress performance.
3. There is little variation among the institutions of public education, and lack of variation limits the ability to affect education performance.	3. There is considerable variation among the public institutions governing education, and this variation affects performance.
4. Bureaucracy is a function of democratic control.	4. Bureaucracy is a function of need.
5. Competition will promote education performance.	5. Competition will promote elitism and de facto segregation.
6. The existing system is incapable of reforms to improve education performance significantly.	6. The existing system can and has made reforms that improve education performance.

This choice, however, seems to risk committing a level of analysis error. The performance of the individual (i.e., the micro level) is being held as evidence of failure in the system (i.e., the macro level). The inherent problems in making such a micro-macro leap have been well documented by social scientists. The institutions themselves are being blamed for poor educational performance, so the institutions should be the primary unit of analysis. This study, therefore, approaches the research questions from a macro level.

Adopting this strategy offers several advantages. First, by avoiding the micro-macro leap, it eliminates the risk of committing the ecological fallacy, that is, using aggregate data to infer the behavior of individuals (Blalock 1964).[7] Second, the macro approach offers a greater opportunity to use objective measures of many variables. Individual-level studies are almost always based on survey data.[8] They include subjective measures—Chubb and Moe, for example, used individuals' perceptions of bureaucracy—which may not be reliable. System-level macro measures, while masking variation among individuals, can be linked to objective phenomena. Third, the macro approach is designed to answer questions on how the system is performing, rather than how individuals are performing and then linking such results to the broader system. This is a more direct route to measuring system performance and capabilities.

While shifting to a macro approach parts company with studies such as Chubb and Moe's, it does not violate the precepts of the institutional theory. Indeed, the institutional theory, with its focus on system organizational structure, seems much more suited to a macro approach than the micro-macro strategies of Chubb and Moe. The macro unit of analysis thus offers both theoretical and practical advantages.

In addition to the macro focus, education systems should be viewed as open systems, their outputs affected by both endogenous and exogenous variables. This is an attempt to clarify, rather than violate, the guidelines laid out by the institutional theory. While Chubb and Moe tend to view organizational characteristics as endogenous, especially regarding the choice between democratic and market control (Tweedie 1990, 550), and are skeptical about the "mysterious" talk of exchanges with external environments, their institutional theory seems to follow an open systems model more than they would like to admit. Their discussion of bureaucracy, for example, clearly indicates the possibility of exogenous influences. Such influences are not unidirectional. An education-related bureaucracy that seeks to address a problem such as teen pregnancy demonstrates that schools are not passive residents within their environments but are actively seeking to change them. Schools are thus seen as organizations involved in complex sets of internal and external relationships that affect their end product (Perrow 1972; Rourke 1984; Thompson 1967).

But adopting an open systems macro approach says more about what will *not* be studied than what will. The system, not the individual, is the unit of analysis—so what is the "system"? Again, this is specified by the institutional theorizing of Chubb and Moe (1990, 5). They say at the heart of the "system" are "the school district and its institutions of democratic control: the school board, the superintendent, and the district office." Above the district, state government is vested with primary control of education under the U.S. Constitution. The state "also has a school board or reasonable facsimile, a superintendent or 'chief state school officer,' and a bureaucracy" (Chubb and Moe 1990, 5).

Above the state is the federal government. Chubb and Moe admit that the federal government's role "by law and custom is distinctly secondary" but that this role has been growing and is supported by a burgeoning bureaucracy.

The institutional theory thus presents three systematic levels of education: district, state, and nation. For a comparative macro approach, the research choices are cross-district, cross-state, and cross-national. In order to be as comprehensive as possible, this study examines all three levels.

District-Level Analysis

District-level data for all public schools in Florida are used for this section of analysis. This data set offers the advantages of a large state with a diverse group of schools and students and provides consistent measures over a number of years.[9] Thus the concepts of interest can be examined both cross-sectionally and longitudinally and on groups of school districts large and diverse enough to support the external validity of any conclusions drawn from the analysis.

A single state is considered an adequate set of districts for a proper test of the institutional theory and school choice. The institutional theory is put forward as a universal model. If the theory finds success in Florida, it will provide preliminary confirmation of the foundational arguments for school choice. If it fails, then the theory's claims collapse entirely. Florida's education system is simply too large for a comprehensive theory of education to dismiss as an anomaly.

Cross-State Analysis

Using the states as units of analysis provides an overall picture of the nation's educational health and allows a comprehensive examination of whether institutional variations can affect performance. Even granting the argument of opponents of democratic control, a national education system simply does not exist in this country. States constitute the largest aggregation of an educational "system" within the United States. Although the federal government has expanded its role in education during the past few decades, the states remain the highest level of government with extensive control over education standards and requirements and provide far more money and administrative support than does the federal government.

The states provide an excellent basis for comparison. Given the variety and number of approaches to education adopted by the states, they make excellent laboratories for examining whether the variation among and reforms adopted by the existing institutional structures make a difference. Because education reform efforts are widespread on this level and presumably designed to affect performance at this level, it is here that the policies of education are most likely to make a difference. If control by political institutions is as detrimental as the institutional theory predicts, the empirical evidence should be found here. This analysis covers all fifty states and both cross-sectional and longitudinal studies are conducted.[10]

Cross-National Analysis

Although America's ability to compete in a global economy is often mentioned as a reason for educational reform, little cross-national comparison of educational systems exists. School choice advocates, certainly Chubb and Moe (1990, 1), use eroding leads in technology and international competition to point out the dangers of a failing education system. Yet in calling for greater local autonomy, school choice advocates pointedly ignore the more centralized education systems of some of America's primary international economic competition. Both Japan and Germany, for example, exert more central government control and more uniformity in education than does the United States. Yet this seems to have done little to hurt them in cross-national studies of student performance.

Owing to data and methodological limitations, analysis at the international level is less sophisticated than at the district and state levels. The most obvious problem with such research is a lack of raw material. Researchers at the Sandia National Laboratories (1992, 288), for example, found "little credible data on international comparisons of education."

Such limitations make sophisticated statistical analysis all but impossible. But even within such constraints, meaningful comparisons can be made. Cross-national performance scores, although limited, are available.[11] Variables such as the presence of national curriculums, the extent of per student funding, and the length of the school year are available. Although lending themselves primarily to descriptive analysis, the available data should provide some clues as to what makes a successful—or unsuccessful—education system.

Conclusion

The most persuasive argument in favor of school choice is the institutional theory laid out by Chubb and Moe. Although criticized, it provides a comprehensive explanatory model of how institutions affect education performance and is a good source of testable hypotheses. Empirical propositions mined from the institutional theory provide the essential tests of the merits of school choice contained in this research. If the relationships predicted by the institutional theory are confirmed, the arguments in favor of school choice gain strong empirical support. If the relationships fail to appear, the institutional theory is wrong and the theoretical support for school choice collapses. Adopting a macro-level, open systems strategy, the institutional theory is put to the test at three systemic levels: district, state, and nation.

Notes

1. More schools did not mean more buildings. Some schools occupy a single floor, although they have their own administrative structure and staff (Henig 1994, 112).
2. Despite relatively low rates of participation, the Minnesota program is one of the most copied in the nation (Henig 1994, 113).
3. Parents certainly have the potential of losing the democratic battle. On any given education issue, however, they are a large percentage of the voting electorate.
4. The point has been amply demonstrated for minorities (see Meier and Stewart 1991).
5. Chubb and Moe thus advocate that bureaucracy is bad but that bureaucrats are not. This contradiction is never fully resolved by the institutional theory.
6. Chubb and Moe, of course, find the problem with democracy is its responsiveness to demands. This same responsiveness is likely to create bureaucracies to solve problems presented to it.
7. Generalizing from one level of analysis to another, however, carries risks regardless of the direction.
8. Chubb and Moe's work is based on two individual-level surveys, the High School and Beyond 1980 Sophomore Cohort First Follow-up, and the High School and Beyond Administrator and Teacher Survey.
9. All data are from the Florida Department of Education and various years of the *Florida Statistical Abstract.* Data availability is a key factor in studying schools; many decentralized school systems simply do not collect the data needed.
10. Data sources for cross-state comparisons include various years of *The Digest of Education Statistics, The Book of the States, Statistical Abstract of the United States,* and other government publications.
11. Such data are collected and reported in various publications of the U.S. Department of Education and the International Education Association.

—————— **Four** ——————

Organization, Competition, and Performance

The institutional theory points to clear relationships between institutional structure and performance. These links provide the strongest theoretical underpinnings of school choice and are an appropriate starting point for an empirical test. As discussed in the previous chapter, support for the role of organization and performance is based in large part on comparisons between public and private schools. Based on research asserting that private schools do a better job of educating their students (Coleman and Hoffer 1987; Coleman, Hoffer, and Kilgore 1982), choice advocates attribute such success to the differing institutional environments of the private and public sectors (Chubb and Moe 1990, 564). Given autonomy and governed by the competition-driven market, private schools respond to the demand for quality education from their primary clientele. Shackled to the demands of broad and competing constituencies, the democratically controlled public schools do not.

This fundamental component of the institutional theory is the basis of many of the empirical propositions listed in Table 3.1 (p. 42). Within the public school system a wealth of data provides ample opportunity to test empirically the claims of the institutional theory about the effects of organization—and even competition—on school performance.[1] The purpose of this chapter is to perform such a test.

Using a district-level data set of Florida public schools, this chapter empirically tests the linkages between organization, competition, and public school performance suggested by the institutional theory. Confirmation of relationships predicted by the institutional theory will lend support for proponents of choice. If such relationships do not appear in the presence of appropriate controls, it will cast doubts on the foundations of the school choice argument and its usefulness as an appropriate policy option for the public school system.

The Florida data set is advantageous for this task for a number of reasons. First, it is detailed and includes variables for all the major concepts needed to test the school choice hypotheses. Second, Florida is a large state with a diverse population. Districts in this data set run the gamut from urban to rural, with different ethnic and socioeconomic compositions. The size and diversity of the sample offer obvious advantages to the validity of the findings reported here.

Organization and Competition

If the institutional theory is correct, then predictable relationships should exist between the organizational attributes and the performance of public schools. Large bureaucracies and greater control by democratic institutions are argued to limit autonomy and should, therefore, be negatively associated with public school performance. Other logical consequences of ineffective organization, such as greater staff turnover and more disciplinary problems, should also exhibit predictable relationships with performance.

Competition, the driving force behind the market solution to improving the education system, is harder to gauge in a public school setting. Indeed, from the perspective of opponents of central control, public education is a quasi monopoly (Peterson 1990) and competition is virtually nonexistent and therefore unmeasurable. The competitive aspect of the market solution promoted by school choice is essentially premised on the idea of exit (Hirschman 1970; see also Lyons, Lowery, and DeHoog 1992). That is, dissatisfaction with the educational quality of one school can result in the exit of a student, who can go elsewhere where standards are higher. The problem with the exit option in a public school system, of course, is the question of where students go when they exit. The options are a private school, if one is available, or a different school jurisdiction. Both require appropriately informed parents with economic resources and a willingness to address transportation or relocation problems.[2]

Still, a reasonable approximation of the effects of competition on public school performance is possible. If a private school and economic resources are available, the exit option is viable, and a competitive situation exists. As argued by school choice advocates, private schools are market driven, and to survive they must attract students who would otherwise attend public schools. In other words, public schools, not other private schools, are the private schools' primary competition. In order to survive, private schools must offer a reason for students to exit the public school system. Although such competition is applicable only to a small section of the student population—those with the appropriate resources—it is nonetheless competition.[3]

Although public school advocates tend to separate public and private schools into distinct environments, such a division is to a great extent artificial. Private schools draw from the same pool of "customers" as public schools do. They must successfully persuade potential public school customers to go private. The lure, according to the institutional theory, is a superior education. For public schools, this is competition at the margins. As the primary supplier of education services, their clientele base is stable. But because socioeconomic advantages are closely associated with academic performance (Coleman et al. 1966), the extent to which private schools are successful in attracting such students has the potential to affect public school performance.

If such competition drives down public school performance, it will indicate a "cream-skimming" effect: private schools will siphon off students with attributes most closely associated with higher educational performance. Such a finding would be quite damaging to the institutional theory and school choice arguments. By compartmentalizing the environments of public and private schools, the institutional theory ignores the fact that private schools are directly engaged in competition with public schools. If such competition can be demonstrated to affect negatively the performance of public schools, the broader consequences are disturbing. If public schools are required to compete against each other, it is unlikely they will all enter the competition as equals. Schools with better records, better facilities, and more resources will have obvious advantages in attracting customers. Given the greater capacities involved (i.e., bigger institutions and more of them), the ability of certain public schools to "cream" will likely vastly outstrip that of private schools. Those public schools entering the educational marketplace competitively handicapped by location or socioeconomics could be devastated.

Market economics dictates that poorly performing schools will improve or close. Closing all of them seems unrealistic—it is highly unlikely there will be enough "good" schools in the short run and perhaps in the long run to accommodate all students in an unpredictable marketplace. What seems more likely is a two-tier system, with certain elite schools benefiting from competition and others hurt as their student populations are hollowed out along with their budgets (Honig 1990–91; U.S. House of Representatives Subcommittee on Elementary, Secondary and Vocational Education 1990).

Nevertheless, if school choice advocates are correct, competition should improve public school performance because competition provides the incentive to improve quality that is lacking in the current system. Within the limited public-private school relationship, this can be empirically studied. If a public school is effectively organized—a condition Chubb and Moe are perfectly willing to admit exists—then it should respond to such competition by improving educational quality.[4] Because many funding programs operate on a per student basis in public schools, they already have an economic motivation to avoid budgetary losses by improving quality.[5] If the competitive link can be associated with higher educational performance in public schools, it will provide strong support for school choice arguments. If competition in the margins of the quasi market between public and private schools is working, there is no apparent reason to assume it would not work in a broader public school setting.

A statistical model with appropriate controls for the exit option, then, should be able to elucidate the consequences of competition in the education marketplace and provide a base empirical test of the institutional theory. Controlling for economic resources and organization attributes, large private school enrollments within a single district should provide evidence of the competition mechanism in action and its consequences for public school performance.[6] This impact should be predictable and significant if the institutional theory is correct. (*Statistically significant,* in the social sciences, commonly means that the probability of an observed statistical relationship being due to chance is less than 5 percent. In other words, in order to declare a relationship significant we must be 95 percent confident that the relationship between two variables is real and not due to random error.)

Data and Methods

Student Performance

Measuring student performance is a controversial topic, with little consensus on the most appropriate method to use (Lehnen 1992; Powell and Steelman 1984; Meyer 1992). Although standardized tests have been criticized with justification, they remain the primary yardstick used by social scientists to measure student and school performance.[7] Such tests remain the most often-used indicator of education performance and quality used by critics of the system.

Students in the Florida education system are required to take a battery of standardized tests in various grades through their school careers. These examinations are designed to test the math and communications skills expected of a student in a given grade. The percentage of students passing these examinations will constitute the dependent variable for the performance model constructed here. A total of six dependent variables are used in this chapter, one for communications and math performance in each of the fifth, eighth, and tenth grades.[8]

Building a model and then using multiple dependent variables measured on the same metric offers several advantages. Repetitive measures offer obvious contributions to the validity of any conclusions drawn from this research. Also, taking comparable measures of different cohorts may offer some insight into whether performance is affected by the same variables in different age groups.

Independent Variables

Organization

Because organizational structure is so crucial to the school choice debate, several variables were used to capture the organizational characteristics of public schools. Bureaucracy is high on the list of Chubb and Moe's symptoms of ineffective organization. Bureaucracies produce and enforce rules and regulations that diminish autonomy and limit the ability of schools to meet demands for educational quality. In short, bureaucracy ensures that the goals of its own constituencies, not the demands of students and parents, are met.

Operationalizing bureaucracy, however, is difficult. As a concept, it is only murkily defined within Chubb and Moe's institutional theory. The hierarchical and rule-enforcing aspects of bureaucracy seem to be the most objectionable (Chubb and Moe 1990, 44–45), but it is often the sheer number of bureaucrats in the public sector that is pointed to as evidence of too much "bureaucracy" (Fliegel and MacGuire

1993, 26–27). Chubb and Moe use perceptions of bureaucracy in their statistical models, but such a measure seems unreliable. What constitutes bureaucratic meddling to one person may be welcome administrative help to another. For our research, bureaucracy was measured as the number of school officials per student.[9] Although aimed only at a single dimension—size—of what is a multidimensional concept, this measure is objective and therefore directly comparable from district to district. It also nicely captures what school choice advocates repeatedly point to as evidence of overbureaucratization—too many bureaucrats. Following the public choice perspective that more bureaucrats equals more bureaucracy, which results in less autonomy, the institutional theory predicts this measure will be negatively related to performance.

While bureaucracy is a problematic symptom, the primary blame for ineffective organization and consequent poor performance is placed by the institutional theory on democratic control. Like bureaucracy, however, "control" is a vaguely defined concept. Comparatively speaking, Florida has a more centralized education system than many other states, with important policy and budget decisions made in Tallahassee, not the local district. Even here, however, there exists a considerable amount of local autonomy. Dade County, for example, has made a concentrated effort to shift decision making downward through a program known as school-based management. While total dollar amounts may be decided elsewhere, how the money is spent is a local decision.

The institutional theory says democratic control is bad for education because it puts decision-making powers under the influence of external constituencies. Following the maxim of the electoral connection, democratic institutions appease whatever constituencies are able to muster a majority over a given question. Systems with democratically elected officials with influence over the decision-making process, therefore, have weaker incentives to fulfill the demands of students and parents. Following the school choice argument, more democracy means more points of access for influence over decision making and weaker incentives to appease students and parents over other constituencies. The greater the degree of democratic control, the worse the effect on educational performance.

The Florida data set allows a straightforward empirical test of this proposition. In Florida, district superintendents can be elected or appointed to their positions. Following the institutional theory, elected superintendents should be responsive to a variety of constituencies other than parents, students, or even the school board. These would include groups influential in their reelection chances, such as teachers' unions and organized groups of property taxpayers. Districts with elected superintendents should be ineffectively organized because individual school autonomy is sacrificed in pursuit of the goals of controlling democratic institution. To test this premise a two-category measure—known as a "dummy variable"—was included, with 1 indicating an elected superintendent and 0 indicating that position was filled by other means.

Within the school system, ineffective organization can be expected to manifest itself in ways besides poor performance. Frustrated teachers are more likely to give up on the system, and students are less likely to respond to it. Consequently, teacher resignations and student disciplinary problems are assumed to be symptoms of ineffective organization. Variables measuring the percentage of school staff resigning and the percentage of the student population receiving disciplinary action were also included in the model. From a school choice perspective, the expected relationships of these variables would be negative. For these variables, no real counterhypothesis to the relationships predicted by school choice theory is available. Few would argue that greater disciplinary problems and more staff turnover promote better education performance. The test of the school choice argument here will come in the impact of these variables in the presence of appropriate controls. As surrogates for ineffective organization, they should show consistent and significant negative relationships with performance.

Competition

Two variables were used to capture the aspects of competition on public school performance. The first measures the percentage of the district's total student population enrolled in private schools. Controlling for economic resources, this variable is used to indicate the viability of the exit option. The greater the viability, the greater the competitive pressure on the public school system to prevent enrollment erosion. If competition works, private school enrollment should be positively associated with public school performance, once appropriate socioeconomic control variables are included. A negative relationship would indicate that competition produces a cream-skimming effect, creating a two-tier system with those who can take advantage of the exit option in the top tier and those who cannot in the lower tier. Such a finding would argue strongly against a market-based educational system by indicating that students with better-informed and better-off parents—attributes strongly associated with performance—will attend one set of schools and those who are disadvantaged will attend another. The poor performing schools of the bottom tier will be economically punished in the market system, even though their students could legitimately be argued to be in greater need of available resources.

The second variable used was the percentage of a district's students enrolled in gifted classes, which was employed as a measure of competitive response. If parents have a realistic exit option, public schools should come under greater pressure to offer programs aimed at boosting the quality of education. Gifted classes are the best education offered by a district, and parents covet such classes for their children (Oakes 1985). The relationship between performance and this variable was expected to be positive.[10]

Control Variables

Student performance is a function of numerous variables beyond the control of the education system. Probably the most important of these are innate cognitive capacity and socioeconomic status (Coleman et al. 1966). Both concepts must be controlled for in order to obtain meaningful interpretations of the impacts of other variables.

The socioeconomic control included is a straightforward measure of mean family income within the district. Because the dependent variable measured one cohort's pass rate on a standardized test, it is possible to control for existing cognitive capacity by including a previous measure of the same cohort's score on the right-hand side of the equation (see Chubb and Moe 1990). Thus in each equation the same cohort's scores from the previous test are included as independent variables.[11] In this manner, nonsystem impacts on performance are controlled for, and changes in the dependent variable must relate to some other source.[12]

Six regression models, each a sophisticated statistical test that uses all of the independent variables to predict the dependent variable, were run—one for each dependent variable.

Findings

Organization

The results of these tests provide little support for the institutional theory and the school choice argument it supports (see appendix, Tables A.1 and A.2, pp. 143 and 144). In many cases the variables designed to test the organization-performance linkages central to the institutional theory had no predictive ability at all. For the most part, the strong relationships predicted by the institutional theory between organization and performance simply failed to appear.

The argument that democratic control is a causal factor of poor performance is contradicted by the failure of the elected superintendent variable to achieve statistical significance in any model. In half the models, not only was the variable insignificant, but it had a positive relationship with the dependent variable—thus indicating that democracy has a *positive* relationship with performance. These results stand in stark contrast to the important effects of democratic control posited by the institutional theory.

The other organizational measures have a mixed impact. The resignation and discipline measures were generally in the direction predicted by the institutional theory, but failed to attain statistical significance in a single model. The failure to achieve statistical significance indicates the relationships are likely the result of random error—that is, pure chance—rather than any meaningful connection between organization and performance. The weak showing of these variables continues to cast doubt on the relationships between organization and performance predicted by the institutional theory.

The most promising organization-related variable for the institutional theory is bureaucracy. With a single exception—the tenth-grade math model (see appendix, Table A.2, p. 144)—it is negatively related with the dependent variables and is often a statistically significant predictor. Based on this variable, large bureaucracies are indeed negatively related to performance. This finding fits with the expectations of the institutional theory.

Competition

The competition variables also had mixed results. Private school participation was negatively related to performance, while participation in gifted classes was positively associated with performance. The private school participation measure was aimed at providing insight into the impact of the exit option. The negative relationship indicates that the presence of a viable exit option—that is, real competition for public schools—drives down public school performance. This finding is important because it adds empirical backing to claims that school choice will effectively result in a two-tier school system. Choice may reward schools that succeed in offering quality education, but it may also leave behind and take resources from schools dealing with the most pressing problems confronting the educational system. In short, the punishment aspect of competition may have severe consequences for those students stuck in the wrong schools. The results here indicate that instead of promoting performance, competition promotes skimming. Simply put, the results indicate that private schools take the students with the characteristics most closely linked to performance. This cream-skimming effect results in the public schools dealing with a greater proportion of students with characteristics negatively associated with performance.[13]

The gifted-class measure was aimed at tapping the dimension of competitive response. The uniform positive direction of the coefficients indicates that public schools have concrete policy options to improve performance. This may not simply be a response to competitive pressure. Gifted classes are a policy option that works even in the absence of high private school enrollments. The stability of the significant coefficients for this variable indicate that for every 1 percentage point increase in students enrolled in gifted classes, there is an increase of 2 percentage points in the number of students passing the math and communication tests. The large impact indicated by these coefficients should be a message of hope to policymakers.[14]

Summary of Findings

Although the relationships posited by school choice advocates by and large failed to appear, all the models were quite powerful, being able to explain anywhere from 46 percent to 68 percent of the variance in education performance. Our findings also support much existing research. As expected, previous test performance was consistently the most powerful predictor of the dependent variable. Interestingly, previous test performance was less influential in the lower grades. Not only were the coefficients large in the tenth-grade models, but previous performance also accounted for a greater proportion of the variance. In the fifth- and eighth-grade models previous test scores tended to account for less than 10 percent of the total variance. In both tenth-grade models the effect of previous test scores was more powerful, accounting for as much as 25 percent of the variance. And in both tenth-grade models, fewer variables were significant predictors of performance. The increasing influence of previous test scores in the higher grades probably accounts for the instability of the coefficients for some of the other variables. The impact of schools on performance seems to be greater in the lower grades. This suggests that any changes in school policy aimed at the high school level may be intervening too late in the process to be effective. School impact on performance is highest at the beginning of a student's school career and then wanes.

The performance of hypotheses derived from the institutional theory is summarized in Table 4.1. As can be seen, the relationships predicted by school choice theory are, overall, unreliable. When an alternative hypothesis exists, school choice predictions perform poorly. Only in the absence of an alternative hypothesis do school choice predictions consistently meet expectations. Only when school choice predictions agree with more broadly accepted organizational determinants of performance do they consistently exhibit relationships in the expected direction. Even here, however, such relationships often fail to achieve statistical significance, indicating the organizational focus of the institutional theory is suspect. The single exception deals with bureaucracy, which consistently meets school choice advocates' expectations of a negative slope and is a statistically significant predictor in two models. Given that this is the only area where public choice expectations have met a measure of success, and the somewhat ambiguous role of bureaucracy within the institutional theory, a closer analysis of bureaucracy is warranted.

Another Look at Bureaucracy

Bureaucracy occupies something of an ambiguous and undefined role in the institutional theory. Chubb and Moe (1990, 63) argue that bureaucracy is an ultimately harmful by-product of control by democratic institutions. They also acknowledge that bureaucracy is promoted by "problem-infested environments." This seems to set up two potential

Table 4.1

Performance of School Choice and Alternative Hypotheses

Variable	School choice predicts	Alternative hypothesis predicts	Times school choice correct	Times alternative correct	Times significant predictor*
Organization					
Size of bureaucracy	–	+	5	1	2
Elected superintendent	–	+	3	3	0
Percentage of staff resigning	–	NA	5	NA	0
Percentage disciplined	–	NA	4	NA	0
Competition					
Percentage of students in private schools	+	–	2	4	4
Percentage in gifted classes	+	NA	6	NA	3

*Indicates met $p < .05$ criterion.

sources of bureaucracy. Bureaucracy is either the outgrowth of democratic control or a function of need or a combination of both.

Chubb and Moe lean toward the first explanation. Bureaucracy is an enforcement mechanism for democratic institutions. As such, it is promoted by democratic control. The counterargument that bureaucracy is a function of need is largely rejected by Chubb and Moe. Others, however, argue that bureaucracy is a useful and appropriate tool to tackle difficult problems. Bureaucracy from this perspective is a response to need (Goodsell 1994).

These opposing viewpoints offer a way to get a more definitive answer on the role of bureaucracy than the inconclusive answers suggested by the performance models. If the institutional theory is correct, bureaucracy should be a function of democratic control. At the least, bureaucracy will be determined by a mix of need and democratic control. If the counterhypothesis is confirmed—that is, if bureaucracy is predominantly a function of need—it will provide evidence that the institutional theory has incorrectly identified the source and role of bureaucracy within the education system.

To test these hypotheses, a model was constructed using the bureaucracy measure as a dependent variable (see appendix, Table A.3, p. 145). Two variables were included to tap the need dimension: the number of schools per capita and the percentage of students enrolled in the free lunch program. A large number of schools should require a greater number of administrators, as the economies of scale involved in larger, centralized schools are not available. The free lunch variable is included as a poverty measure. A host of education problems are associated with poverty (Kozol 1991); and if bureaucracy is a response to need, there should be more bureaucrats administering the appropriate programs where such problems exist. Both measures are positively related to the size of bureaucracy and support the need hypothesis. The positive slope of schools per capita highlights what appears to be an irony in the school choice argument, which calls for more schools and less bureaucracy. This may be asking the impossible. While hierarchical layers of bureaucracy may be stripped, each school requires an administrative staff. More schools therefore equal more bureaucracy.

Two variables were included to test the institutional theory's predictions on the source of bureaucracy. An elected superintendent was included as a measure of democratic control, which, following Chubb and Moe's argument, should be strongly positively correlated with the size of bureaucracy. It is not. An elected superintendent is negatively associated with bureaucracy, indicating that democratic control and bloated bureaucracy do not go hand in hand. This finding is important because it lends support to an argument that democratic control and bureaucracy are distinct theoretical and empirical concepts. While the institutional theory melds the two, the hypotheses on their relationships with educational outputs seem to be grounded more in normative perceptions than empirical reality.

Average teacher salary was included in the model as a surrogate measure of teachers' organizational strength. Districts with more highly organized teachers' groups should be able to translate that strength into dollars. School choice advocates generally agree that teachers' unions constitute a primary client for the education bureaucracy. If the institutional theory is correct, the salary measure should be positively associated with bureaucracy. Again, the relationship is in the opposite direction predicted by the institutional theory. Far from contributing to the size of bureaucracy, teacher organizational strength apparently limits it.[15] As a control, per student expenditures were included in the model as a measure of available resources. The positive relationship indicates that bureaucracy is also a function of the financial strength of the district.

Overall, this model had impressive predictive power (explaining 78 percent of the variation in bureaucracy) and raised severe doubts about the role and source of bureaucracy posited by the institutional theory. Contrary to school choice theory expectations, bureaucracy is a function neither of democratic control nor of the organizational strength of teachers. Instead, large bureaucracies seem to be driven by need. While it could be claimed that the positive slope of the expenditure variable is evidence of the budget-maximizing nature of bureaucrats (Niskanen 1971), the performance of other variables in the model limits the extent and impact of such an argument. Bureaucracy, it appears, is not the problem its public choice critics suggest. The relationship between bureaucracy and performance shown in the performance models may thus be misleading. It may not be bureaucracy itself that is suppressing performance, but other "need" variables, such as poverty, that are associated with bureaucracy.

Conclusion

An initial test of the empirical propositions suggested by the institutional theory raises severe doubts about school choice. When faced with a counterhypothesis, none of the predictions drawn from the institutional theory about the relationship between organization, competition, and performance materializes. Instead, existing cognitive capacity and gifted classes prove to be the best predictors of performance. Both findings support existing research.

Most important for the school choice debate, competition between public and private schools appears to result in a cream-skimming effect. There seems to be no reason to argue that such effects would disappear in competition among public schools, especially as some schools would begin with competitive advantages. This indicates that an educational market may result in a two-tier system and exacerbate the already considerable inequities among school districts.

These findings cast doubt on the foundations of the school choice argument. The organizational perspective that stands at the core of the institutional theory has not withstood this initial empirical test, indicating public choice advocates have at least partially misidentified the problems they seek to correct.

Notes

1. Chubb and Moe do several empirical analyses to support the relationships predicted by the institutional theory, including those dealing with organization and performance. These models are detailed in Appendix D of their book (1990, 259–77). The predictive power of their models on student achievement gains, however, is disappointing, with reported adjusted R-squares of less than .05.

2. As reported in previous chapters, this is not a trivial concern. Geographical location, especially, is a prime determinant of where parents send their children to school (Elmore 1990).

3. The theory operates at the margins. For most public school students, a combination of factors makes school transfers unlikely. At the margins are students with the resources and opportunity to make choice among education institutions—public or private—a reality.

4. Chubb and Moe do not argue that there are no effectively organized public schools. Effectively organized public schools, however, are less likely because of the organizational structure that governs them. See Chubb and Moe (1990, 60–61).

5. Florida uses a state-mandated formula based on enrollment and educational costs to fund local school districts.

6. Within the data set used here private school enrollments can account for a significant portion of the student population—as high as 15 percent in some districts.

7. A persistent problem with standardized tests is that they include a component of random error. Correct answers can be a result of knowledge or simply a

guess. Determining the size of the random error component and controlling for it is, needless to say, difficult in the extreme. The analyses of Chubb and Moe also rely on standardized test data.

8. All education data were supplied by the Florida Department of Education. All noneducation data were gathered from the *Florida Statistical Abstract*. All data are for 1988 unless otherwise noted.

9. School officials are employees who work in the central administrative apparatus. The category does not include principals, assistant principals, or any support personnel such as teachers aides, bus drivers, or food service workers.

10. Again, there is no counterhypothesis to the relationship predicted by the institutional theory. Greater participation in gifted classes should not suppress performance. The idea here is to give a full test of the competition mechanism. If private school enrollments go up, we should see an appropriate response by public schools to this competitive pressure.

11. The tests are administered in the third, fifth, eighth, and tenth grades. Thus when the fifth grade's 1988 scores were used as a dependent variable, the same cohort's third-grade (1986) scores were included as independent variables.

12. The full model is specified thus:

$$PERF = b_1 BUR + b_2 SUP + b_3 DIS + b_4 RES + b_5 PRI + b_6 GIF + b_7 PASS + b_8 INC$$

Where:

PERF = performance measured as percentage of students passing 1988 stan-
dardized math or communications test.
PRI = private school enrollment, measured as a percentage of a district's
total student population attending private schools.
BUR = bureaucracy, measured as number of school officials per student.
SUP = a dummy variable with 1 indicating superintendent is an elected posi-
tion, 0 indicating position is filled by other means.
DIS = percentage of students disciplined.
RES = percentage of district staff resigning.
GIF = percentage of students enrolled in gifted classes.
PASS = cohort's pass rate on the previous test.
INC = mean family income within the district.

A total of six regression models were run, one for each dependent variable. Regression diagnostics were examined for each model. The sixty-seven school districts in this study represent a relatively small *N*, which can produce distortions owing to extreme cases and non-Gaussian data. Dummy variables for individual school districts were included when large studentized residuals indicated those districts were having a disproportionate impact on the regression. Because of missing data, not all school districts are included in every regression.

13. Because empirical claims of a creaming effect from competition are such a strong challenge to public choice, a two-stage least-squares analysis was done to reexamine the causal links between private school attendance and public school performance.

In the first stage, two regression models were constructed, one to predict private school attendance, one to predict public school performance. As most private schools are Catholic, and attending private school requires financial resources, the percentage of Catholics and mean family income were used to predict private school attendance within a school district. Public school performance (measured as the percentage passing standardized tests) was predicted by a cohort's previous pass rate, the percentage of students in gifted classes, and the percentage of students disciplined. The residuals were saved from each model and were included in the second stage to examine the relationship between performance and private school attendance.

For all six performance measures (i.e., the six dependent variables used for the model), the relationships were strongly negative and significant. As public school performance increased, private school attendance decreased. As private school attendance increased, public school performance decreased.

This analysis accomplished two goals. First, it provided empirical backing to the argument pursued in this chapter that a competitive relationship exists between private and public schools. Private school attendance and public school performance fluctuated as one would expect in a quasi-market situation. Second, the results added confidence to the inference of a creaming effect. As private schools attract more students, the performance of public schools suffers. Although the two-stage least-squares model was relatively simple, the consistency of the results across the performance measures lends support to the competitive relationships and the resulting creaming effect argued to exist in this chapter.

14. Such a message should be treated with caution. Previous research has shown that there are important questions about equity in separating students into ability groups. Specifically, minorities are underrepresented in gifted classes and overrepresented in remedial classes (Meier and Stewart 1991; Meier, Stewart, and England 1989).

15. This makes sense. Teachers should have no interest in bureaucracies that restrict their teaching autonomy.

———— Five ————

Private Schools:
The Chicken or the Egg?

Although severely damaging to the institutional theory, the results presented in chapter four are not necessarily fatal. School choice advocates can salvage, and perhaps even take comfort from, the findings on competition. The skimming effect uncovered by the previous analysis adds empirical support to charges that school choice promotes elitism but does not demonstrate that competition fails to promote quality. Nothing thus far indicates that students are exiting the public school system for any other reason than the chance of a superior education. Although serious normative questions are raised about the possibility of a two-tier education system, the demand assumption and the perceived benefits of competition central to the institutional theory are not empirically contradicted.

School choice arguments draw much of their strength from the idea that private schools fulfill an unmet demand for quality education. Controlled by the marketplace, private schools must meet the demands of their primary clientele in order to survive. Proponents argue that private schools are organized around this central goal (Chubb and Moe 1990, 181–83). This organizational structure is the key difference between the public and private education sectors. The institutional environment of public schools is geared toward meeting the demands of numerous constituencies. Private schools, in contrast, are forced by the competitive market to focus on delivering a quality education.

The market is portrayed as the savior of public education. If regulation is ceded from democratic institutions to the market, public schools will mimic private schools. They will focus on meeting the demands of their primary clientele. The primary demand of both students and parents, posits the institutional theory, is a quality education. Private schools can deliver this quality, and public schools cannot.

The demand assumption is just that, an assumption. No proof exists that parents' primary demand is for quality education. The advocates assume that private schools do better because they respond to this demand for quality. School choice advocates see that private schools are slightly superior academically to public schools and assume that the reason is competition. This perspective draws support from research showing private school students score higher on achievement tests (Coleman and Hoffer 1987; Coleman, Hoffer, and Kilgore 1982) and from the modest differences found by Chubb and Moe (1990). Some evidence, however, suggests that the reason for such success is not necessarily the superior education offered by private schools.

Private school students are more likely to have the attributes (notably high socioeconomic status) associated with achievement than their public school counterparts. The students are more likely to come from stable homes with middle-class values and incomes. After all, private schools charge tuition, and some families cannot afford the fees. Private schools also do not admit all students who apply; they engage in an admissions process that screens out students who carry the risk of academic failure (see, e.g., Witte 1992).[1] Two selection mechanisms thus provide a student body for most private schools that is different from that of public schools. The market pricing system eliminates some students who would be difficult to educate, and the school's admission procedures screen out the rest.

The contention that private schools service a demand for quality education is undercut by the modest differences between public and private school students. Chubb and Moe (1990) found private school students on average answered correctly only one-half a question more than their public school cohorts. If a quality demand were the sole driving force behind private schools, surely such differences would be larger, especially given the private school students' more favorable socioeconomic status.

The causal link between academic success and competition represented by the assumption demand, in other words, is a theoretical axiom with little empirical support. This chapter answers the question whether the relationships surrounding the demand assumption function as well in the empirical world as they do in theory.

A List of Demands

The institutional theory assumes a demand for quality education, a demand that private schools are better able to meet than public schools.

Markets for any product, however, rarely focus on a single goal. They frequently offer products of different colors, sizes, and quality. Quality education, therefore, is probably only one of a list of possible demands private schools seek to meet. If private schools lack a laserlike focus on quality education and instead seek to fulfill a broad range of demands, the link between competition and a better system of education is weakened.

An obvious educational demand is the demand for religious education. The courts have enforced a strict secularism on public schools. Few issues are as emotional as school prayer and Bible reading. Parents who want their children to get an education that reflects their religious beliefs have no option but private schools. Services based around religion, not quality, constitute a large reason for the demand for private school education (Brown 1992). This demand explains why the vast majority of private schools have some sort of religious affiliation. Religion and a quality education are certainly not incompatible concepts. The introduction of religion-based education as a demand that private schools attempt to meet, however, dampens the consequences of the competitive market mechanism that school choice advocates envision.

Another parental demand on schools is simple geographical proximity. Much of the school choice literature assumes that all parents will become knowledgeable, informed consumers in an education marketplace and will make cost-benefit decisions centered on a better educational product. The theory works only to the degree that parents fit the assumptions of the classical rational consumer. Many parents do not think of education as similar to buying a car; but if they do, they are likely to seek a product that meets a variety of goals. Where choice systems have been enacted, getting the appropriate information to parents has proven to be a logistic and financial burden that has scored only mixed success (Carnegie Foundation 1992, 49; Chriss, Nash, and Stern 1992). Most parents do know the geographic location of the school nearest their home. This information and the convenience it represents seem to be the largest factor in choosing a school (Elmore 1990, 306). Just as convenience stores flourish by offering longer hours and closer proximity (although at higher prices), convenient schools also flourish. Most parents like their children to attend neighborhood schools.

Less benign potential demands may also be met in the educational marketplace. Elitism is one of the strongest criticisms leveled against a system based on choice (Honig 1990–91). Segregation may also be a demand competitors in the education market may find profitable to pursue. Freedom to choose where and with whom children went to school, after all, was the primary defense of segregation. The initial post-*Brown* freedom-of-choice plans generally failed to desegregate schools (see Rodgers and Bullock 1976). At the present time a public school is legally prevented from de jure segregation. A private school, unfettered by an open-enrollment mandate, may be able to use a selective admissions policy to produce a segregated student body. Currently, as a percentage of enrollment, minorities are twice as likely to attend public than private schools (Witte 1992).[2]

A long list of other demands for education can be enumerated: the quality of athletics and other extracurricular activities, the desire to attend a school with a diverse student body, the availability of special curricula or specialized classes, family traditions of attending a school, the available social development opportunities, and so on.

We are not arguing that educational quality is of no consequence in choosing a private over a public school. All real-world markets provide a variety of goods; consumers can rationally select goods of lower quality if that good meets other needs. Not everyone would purchase a Mercedes even if price were not a constraint; many would still opt for Yugos. An education market would be similar. Educational quality, therefore, may be a demand of parents and students; but this brief discussion indicates it may not be the only, or even the primary, demand.

Testing the Causal Link

The demand assumption posits a causal link between educational quality and private school attendance. Once resources are taken into consideration, then private school enrollment should be a function of demand for quality education. Evidence of that demand can be found in public school performance. If public schools are performing well, that is, if they are fulfilling demand, parents have no reason to seek out the private school alternative. Public school systems with good records of academic success should depress the demand for private education. Public school systems with poor records should do the opposite.

This proposition also reintroduces the issue of cream skimming. If private schools take the students with the best chance of academic success, then public school performance should fluctuate with private school enrollment. As private school enrollments become larger, public school performance should suffer. This flow of causality is the reverse of that reasoned by the demand assumption and represents the counterhypothesis.

The analysis in chapter four presented some evidence to support the effect of creaming, but a cross-sectional model is a poor platform from which to assert causality. Three conditions are set as tests of causality: temporal order (i.e., if X causes Y, it must precede it temporally); association (X and Y vary together); and control (other likely causes of Y are controlled for; see Blalock 1964). This research question is particularly suited to a pooled model that combines the advantages of cross-sectional and time-series analysis (Stimson 1985).

Testing and the Demand Assumption

Research Design

We use two models with school districts as units of analysis to examine the relationships between public school performance and private school enrollment. Using an expanded version of the Florida data set employed in chapter four, public school performance is measured as the percentage of students passing the standardized tenth-grade math and communications tests. Private school enrollment is measured as a percentage of a district's total student population attending private schools. These constitute the dependent variables for the study.

For each model, we control for previous values of the dependent variables; that is, the model for private school enrollment contains a measure of private school enrollment in the previous year. This is known as lagging the dependent variable and accomplishes two goals. First, lagging the dependent variable makes it difficult for any other variable to demonstrate a significant relationship. All organizations exhibit a great deal of inertia; next year they will look a lot like this year. Schools are no exception to this rule. Including a lagged dependent variable helps accomplish the control condition of causality; it represents all the factors that contribute to organizational inertia. Second, it provides the temporal test of causality. In essence this design is set up to answer a chicken and egg question (Thurman and Fisher 1988). In research that examines the same group of subjects over time (this sort of study is known as panel analysis), a straightforward set of conditions is used to infer causality. X is said to cause Y if X at time t minus 1 is correlated with Y at time t (Hsiao 1986). In other words, in order to claim that X causes Y, X has to come first. If the egg shows up first, we take that to mean the egg caused the chicken.[3]

If the demand assumption is correct, then in the private school enrollment model the lagged public school performance variable should be a negative and significant predictor. As the public school system's performance declines, students should move to private schools in order to satisfy demand for quality education, once economic resources are controlled for. If the cream-skimming hypothesis is correct, the reverse flow of causality should appear. In this instance, the lagged private school enrollment variable should be a negative and significant predictor of public school performance. As good students transfer from public to private schools, the performance level in public schools will decline.

Controls

Private School Enrollment Model

Several other variables are included in this model to control for other potential causes of private school enrollments. The first control is the percentage of district residents who are Catholic. Catholic schools are by far the dominant form of private education, and they offer religious services unavailable in public schools. Areas with large Catholic populations are more likely to demand such services and support Catholic schools and thus high private school enrollments.[4]

A second control variable is the percentage of public school enrollment that is black. A persistent criticism of school choice is that it will promote segregation. After all, the South witnessed an explosive growth in private schools after the courts required public schools to desegregate (Henig 1994, 102). Advocates dismiss such criticisms, arguing that minorities will benefit from choice because it will allow them access to the better education opportunities in the mostly white suburbs. This variable is designed to test to what extent those attending private schools are purchasing segregation rather than quality education. If segregation is a desired commodity, then private school enrollments should rise as black public school enrollments increase. If this variable is a significant and positive predictor, it will provide important support for the argument that a choice system will be elitist. School choice advocates present private schools as a model to be emulated. If that model facilitates segregation, it raises a powerful normative argument against choice.[5]

Finally, mean family income is included to control for economic resources. The decision to attend private school must be accompanied by the ability to pay for it. This variable is designed to allow a realistic examination of what causes private school attendance when the influence of money is removed.

Public School Performance Model

This model is based on that used in chapter four, but is respecified to reflect the findings of that analysis and to accommodate the focus of inquiry here. A cohort's previous performance on examinations, the percentage of students in gifted classes, and family income were all shown to be important predictors of system performance in the chapter four model. Accordingly, these variables are incorporated into this model as controls. All should be positive indicators of performance. In addition, we need a measure of students with special problems and needs. Some schools succeed not because they have done a good job but because their students would succeed in any environment. Poverty is associated with a wide variety of educational needs and problems. The variable, the percentage of students in a district's free lunch program, seeks to control for pockets of poverty that may not be reflected in the family income variable.

The variable of most interest in this model is lagged private school enrollment, which provides the test of the cream-skimming hypothesis. The lagged performance measure also has an important control function. It represents the historical educational performance of a school district.[6] Schools with records of high educational performance are more likely to repeat that success than those with poor records.[7]

The private school enrollment model was applied to a pooled data set that contains all Florida school districts from 1986 to 1990. The public school performance model was applied to a pooled data set inclusive of all Florida school districts from 1988 to 1990.[8] In each case two versions of each model were run—one using the pass rates on the math test as a public school performance variable, one using pass rates on the communications test.[9]

Why Do Students Attend Private Schools?

Since we have two measures of student performance—test results for math and for communications—we run two models predicting the level of private school enrollment. The most important factor is inertia. School districts with large private school enrollments generally had large private school enrollments the year before. What about the performance of public schools? The school choice demand assumption holds that the lower the performance of public school students, the greater the demand for private schooling will be.

The actual results diverge from the school choice argument (see appendix, Tables A.4, A.5, pp. 145 and 146). Student math scores are actually positively related to private school enrollments; however, the relationship is so small that it cannot be considered substantively or statistically significant. Similarly, public school student performance on the communications examination is unrelated to private school enrollments. Private school enrollments do not increase as the performance of public schools declines.

If students do not attend private school because public schools fail to meet the demand for quality education, why do they attend? Our models show that two factors other than inertia are important: religion and race. As the percentage of Catholic population increases, student enrollment in private schools also increases. Similarly, as black student enrollment in public schools increases, total enrollment in private schools also increases.[10] The results suggest that people are not buying quality education from private schools. They are instead purchasing religious services and racial segregation.[11]

The results offer strong evidence that school choice advocates have seriously misjudged the relationship between public school performance and what is offered in the private education marketplace. Needless to say, such findings stand in stark contrast to the expectations of the demand assumption. Perhaps, however, one year is not a long enough time period to see the changes predicted by the school choice model. After all it takes time to move a student to another school and time for private schools to expand to accommodate increased demands. To see if this was true, we increased the lag length for the previous private school enrollment to two years, three years, and four years (see appendix, Table A.6, p. 146).

Because the longer lags give the other explanatory variables more time to have an impact, we should not be surprised that the relationships increase. In the case of black student enrollment and Catholic population, the relationships strengthen. After four years, the black enrollment in the public system has three times the impact that it had after one year. After four years, the influence of Catholic population is four times what it was after only a single year. The increasing strength of the coefficients reflects a delay between an influx of minorities into the public school system and the resulting exit of whites. In other words, at the present time (in contrast to the period immediately following desegregation) whites exit the public school system gradually in response to increased minority enrollment, not in a sudden rush.

The analysis shows no indication at all that public school performance plays any significant role in private school attendance. In the few instances where the performance measures are significant, the slopes are positive. That is, private school enrollments increase as the performance of public schools improves. This completely contradicts the relationship predicted by the institutional theory. Whatever is motivating people to attend private schools, it appears to have nothing to do with poorly performing public schools.

In sum, the results of the private school enrollment model find nothing to support an argument that there is a causal link between poor public school performance and private school attendance. Yet the variables measuring black percentage of public school enrollment and a district's Catholic population both meet the parameters laid down to infer causality. Exiting the public school system appears to have nothing to do with the system's academic record. The causal link is instead grounded in demand for religious services and segregation. These findings undermine a key support for the institutional theory and contradict arguments that a choice system will see enrollment shifts based on movement toward more attractive educational opportunities. In the education marketplace, offering religious services and segregation may be just as profitable as offering an education demonstrably superior to the competition's alternative.

What Determines Public Student Performance?

We then looked at the results on the public school performance model (see appendix, Tables A.7, A.8, p. 147). Inertia has a performance element both at the individual level and at the system level. Student groups that have done well in the past will continue to do well; school systems that have records of good performance will continue those records.

The models provide evidence to support the cream-skimming effect reported in chapter four. Lagged private school enrollment is negatively related to public school performance. As private schools take the students with the best chance of academic success, public school performance suffers. In the communications model, for example, the coefficient estimates an increase of 4 percentage points in private school enrollment is associated with a decrease of 1 percentage point in public school performance in the following year.[12]

Interestingly, the lagged performance variable is as important as the cohort's previous pass rate. This indicates that public schools with a history of good academic performance show good results independent of the demonstrated cognitive capacity of their students. In other words, schools matter. They contribute to the performance of their students. The results show strong support for the cream-skimming effect. While public school performance showed no sign of influencing private school enrollment, private school enrollment shows definite signs of influencing public school performance. The flow of causality indicated in these models strongly suggests the demand assumption is at best seriously flawed.

Again to get a better picture of the process of student performance, we increased the lag length on the performance variable to two, three, and four years (see appendix, Table A.9, p. 148). Again, the coefficients were stable across time and the performance of the private school enrollment variable meets the criteria established to infer causality.

The coefficients also indicate that relationships between private school attendance and public school performance increase with time. This probably reflects the "hollowing out" effect of exit from the public school system. As private schools skim the best and the brightest, the number of academically successful students left in the public school system slowly declines, resulting in an ever-increasing impact on public school performance.

The control variables of percentage of students in gifted classes, percentage of students receiving free lunches, and (in both models) mean family income have no discernible impact on the dependent variables. The coefficients are small and are not statistically significant. The failure of these variables almost certainly results from the inclusion of the lagged version of the dependent variable on the right-hand side of the equation. This is in effect acting as a supercontrol variable, accounting for all effects that were present during previous years.

Confirming Performance Patterns

The segregationist aspects uncovered in the private school enrollment models raise the question whether racial patterns also exist in the determinants of public school performance. If minority enrollment drives whites away from the public school system, is it possible there are differences in patterns of black and white academic performance within the public system?[13]

In order to test this proposition a series of performance models were constructed to look at the differences between black and white students. The models are specified the same as the broader public performance model and applied to the same pooled data set, the only exceptions being that the academic performance variables are race specific.[14]

One important difference between the race-specific and broader performance models should be noted: we did not use all the Florida school districts. Only districts with an enrollment that was at least 15 percent black were included. The reason for setting this minimum was that a number of districts had small total enrollments that included only a few black students. This meant a change of as little as four fewer black students passing the math or communications tests resulted in large swings in the dependent variable. Such results are obviously misleading.

The results of the race-specific performance models generally confirm the patterns evident in the broader models (see appendix, Tables A.10, A.11, p. 149). Again the most important predictors of performance are the cohort's pass rate on the previous test and the historical performance record of the district. Also, the control variables of percentage in gifted classes, percentage receiving free lunches, and mean family income once again fail to achieve statistical significance.

Two important differences between the race-specific and broader performance models are evident. First, the private school enrollment variable is not a significant predictor in either the math or the communications model. Second, in general the race-specific models do not predict as accurately as the general model.

Both differences almost certainly share the same explanation: the fraction of total enrollment blacks and whites represent in many districts. Because this fraction in many cases is quite small, the race-specific models are attempting to explain variation based on a much smaller population than the broader models.[15] Even more important is the relative lack of variation within these smaller, ethnically concentrated populations. Performance on the standardized tests is much more stable within and across districts when examined by individual ethnic group than when all students are considered together.

This lack of variation does two things. First, it points out the well-established differences among racial groups in regard to success on standardized tests. These differences probably have as much to do with socioeconomics as with race. As a group, blacks are socioeconomically less well off than whites. Because socioeconomic advantage is associated commonly with academic success (Coleman et al. 1966), it is not surprising to find differences based on race. The second effect of less variation is that there is less for the model to explain. The weaker performance of the race-specific models is thus not surprising.

Although the models show similar patterns of academic performance for both ethnic groups, there are some interesting differences. These differences show up best when we increase the lag length of the dependent variables to two, three, and four years (see appendix, Tables A.12, A.13, pp. 150 and 151). The cohort's previous pass rate appears to have a larger impact on black performance than on white. Also, percentage in gifted classes has a significant impact on white performance, but not on black performance. This may reflect patterns of discrimination in the delivery of education services within the public school system. Previous research has shown that whites tend to be overrepresented in gifted and talented classes, while minorities are overrepresented in remedial classes (Meier, Stewart, and England 1989). Florida is no exception to this pattern. Blacks may have to rely more on their own cognitive resources and less on the assistance of the education system than whites do.

Conclusion

The results presented in this chapter show strong support for the cream-skimming hypothesis and nothing to support the demand assumption. The findings contradict an important component of the institutional theory and thus undercut several key school choice arguments.

The institutional theory is built on the assumption that private schools survive by offering a better educational product than the public alternative. People with the appropriate resources seek to satisfy their demand for quality education by exiting the public education system. Building on this assumption, choice advocates argue that introducing competition among public schools will have the beneficial effect of promoting quality. By extending the opportunity to seek a better education to all income groups, the public school system will respond to a competitive market in much the same way that private schools already do.

The results presented here, however, indicate that private schools may attract customers by offering religious services and racial segregation. If public schools will respond to a competitive market in the same fashion as private schools—the perspective favored by public choice advocates—the normative questions raised are considerable. Do we want schools attracting students based on the religious content of their curriculum or the racial composition of their enrollment? If public schools do indeed respond to competition in the same fashion as private schools, it seems not only possible but probable that some schools will do exactly that. And they will do it for the very reasons choice advocates argue will promote a more beneficial system: economic survival in a competitive market.

To say parochial schools offer a religion-based curriculum that is attractive to many parents is a fairly noncontroversial statement. Finding a religious component linked to the success of Catholic schools in attracting new students is hardly breaking new ground. Catholic schools, after all, do not seek to hide their religious affiliation. To parents dissatisfied with the secular nature of public schools, such schools offer obvious advantages. The academic successes of Catholic schools have been well documented, and for a parent with the resources and the religious inclination, the question seems to be not why send a child to a parochial school, but why not? There is no reason to assume the clientele of non-Catholic parochial schools is motivated for different reasons.

The findings on segregation are much more controversial. School choice advocates, using the private schools as a model, consistently deny charges that a market-regulated education system will be elitist. As evidence, choice advocates can point to research indicating private schools are as racially diverse as public schools (e.g., Bryk and Lee

1992; but see Witte 1992). The results presented here, however, raise serious questions about the potential of a competitive system to increase segregation. If public schools within such a system will act much as private schools currently do—as choice advocates argue— then these results strongly suggest that segregation will be one of the demands driving the market. Choice seems to have a real potential to exacerbate the already considerable problems of de facto segregation in the public school system.

Serious questions are also raised about using public money to fund schools that respond to market demands for religious services or segregation. A school choice system may be able to solve this problem to some extent by suppressing such demands through force of law. This would not only require enforceable legislation but the acceptance of a deep irony. To prevent the excesses of a choice system, it would have to rely on the very institutional structures—control by democratic bodies and regulation through bureaucracy—that it seeks to eliminate.

The cream-skimming finding is equally devastating for the public choice model. It suggests that private school performance is a function of limiting inputs by restricting access to the best and most educable students. Schools find it fairly easy to educate white middle-class students from stable families; it is much more difficult to educate poor, racially diverse students from broken families. Additional support for the cream-skimming hypotheses can be found in the Milwaukee school choice experiment. In that experiment, private schools cannot cream; if they agree to participate in the program, they must take all students assigned to them. In addition, only school-lunch-eligible students can participate in the choice program. As a result, the elite private schools in the Milwaukee area have refused to participate in the program. If they have to play on a level playing field, the private schools opt not to play.

The empirical dismantling of the institutional theory's demand assumption therefore raises serious doubts about the promised benefits of choice. With no guarantee that demand for quality education would drive a competitive market, choice rapidly runs into normative obstacles. It would seem unlikely that a system proposing to funnel public money to organizations that have to respond to religious or racial demands to survive could get much public support. Yet the results here indicate the popular policy reform of school choice may do exactly that.

Notes

1. Witte's argument deals with Catholic, as opposed to all private, schools. Since Catholic schools constitute the majority of private schools, this generalization is not seen as doing too much violence to Witte's more focused argument.

2. Based on the high school and beyond data, Witte reports that blacks and Hispanics made up 10.9 percent of private school enrollments and 20.8 percent of public school enrollments. Handicapped students made up 1.5 percent of private school enrollments and 4.9 percent of public school enrollments.

3. The methodology employed here is based on previous work (Meier and Smith 1994) used to examine the causal links among politics, bureaucracy, and minority employment.

4. Despite a large Hispanic population, Florida is not an especially Catholic state.

5. See the extensive literature on "white flight" referenced in Meier, Stewart, and England (1989).

6. It should be clear that the cohort's previous pass rate and the lagged version of the dependent variable are not the same thing. The previous pass rate represents the percentage of the cohort who passed the eighth-grade test. The lagged version of the dependent variable represents how many students passed the tenth-grade test at $t-1, t-2$, etc.

7. The fully specified models are as follows.

Private school enrollment model:

$$PRI = b_1LPRI + b_2LPERF + b_3PBSTUD + b_4CATH\% + b_5INC$$

Public school performance model:

$$PERF = b_1PASS + b_2LPERF + b_3LPRI + b_4GIF + b_5INC + b_6FREELUN$$

Where:

PRI	=	private school enrollment measured as a percentage of total district enrollment attending private schools.
PERF	=	public school performance measured as a percentage of students passing standardized tenth-grade math or communications tests.
LPRI	=	lagged private school enrollment (i.e., PRI at $t-1$).
LPERF	=	lagged public school performance (i.e., PERF at $t-1$).
PBSTUD	=	percentage of district enrollment that is black.
CATH%	=	percentage of district residents who are Catholic.
INC	=	mean district family income.
GIF	=	percentage of students in gifted classes.
PASS	=	cohorts pass rate on previous test.
FREELUN	=	percentage of students receiving free lunches.

8. Missing data prevented including more time points in the public school performance model.

9. Pooled designs often require substantial statistical manipulation to over-

come the methodological challenges inherent in the technique. In this instance, however, the approach is fairly straightforward. An OLS design was considered appropriate because the models contain lagged dependent variables as predictors and because the design is unit (i.e., cross-sectional) rather than time dominant (see Stimson 1985). In some models dummy variables for years were included as controls for autocorrelation, and dummy variables for individual school districts were included where diagnostics indicated outliers. In general, when such corrective controls are made, diagnostics show neither autocorrelation nor heteroskedasticity to be at unacceptable levels in the final models (see Stimson 1985; Hsiao 1986, chap. 4). The single exception was the public school performance model using the math-based performance variable. Even after employing year dummies, diagnostics indicated autocorrelation in this model was high enough to make the estimates unreliable. Accordingly, to correct for autocorrelation in this model it was necessary to use a generalized least-squares technique, and GLS coefficients are reported.

10. The use of a lagged dependent variable means the impacts shown in the table are for the first year only. The increase in private school enrollment in the first year is then built into the value of the lagged dependent variable for the second year. This results in the impact of the independent variable being distributed over time in a geometrically distributed lag (Pindyck and Rubinfeld 1991). The total impact over time of the variable is equal to the original slope divided by 1 minus the slope of the lagged dependent variable. The total impact of the black enrollment variable for a 1 percentage point change is .117 as the change works its way through the system of equations over time. As we lengthen the lag for the dependent variable below, we will see this increase in impact.

11. Both versions of the enrollment model explain virtually all the variance in the dependent variable and show no evidence of contamination from autocorrelation. The reported estimated Rho is an autocorrelation diagnostic. If the Rho is insignificant or below .2, OLS is considered a superior estimation technique. The coefficients for both models are virtually the same, indicating the variables based on math and communications tests are measuring the same dimension of education. As expected, the lagged version of the dependent variable is strongly significant in both models and explains much of the variance, forcing other variables in the model to meet a high threshold in order to demonstrate significant relationships.

12. The total impact over time as mediated through the lagged dependent variable is .423 points for every 1 percentage point of private school enrollment. See note 10.

13. Minority enrollment was not included as a determinant of public school performance for several reasons. Primary among these is that there is no reason to assume minorities are inherently less likely to succeed academically than whites. It is almost certainly socioeconomics—controlled for in the model—that causes the academic performance of minorities to trail that of whites. Skin pigment by itself is a theoretically indefensible—not to mention repugnant—explanation of academic performance.

14. Again, where diagnostics indicated they were necessary, dummy variables for individual years were included to control for autocorrelation.

15. Florida's large Hispanic population means that in many districts whites may be a minority.

—————— **Six** ——————

Politics and Performance

The institutional theory has thus far been a poor explanatory model. Of the empirical propositions drawn from Chubb and Moe's reasoning, those dealing with demand, democratic control, bureaucracy, and competition (propositions 1, 2, 4, and 5 in Table 3.1, p. 42) have failed to meet school choice advocates' expectations. While the counterhypotheses suggested by school choice critics are not joined in a cohesive structure such as the institutional theory, they have so far proved to be the more robust explanatory platform.

Still, the school choice cargo carried by the institutional theory has not yet been lost. Two of the six empirical propositions—those dealing with institutional variation and reform—have not been directly addressed. The argument that the public school system has uniform, monopolistic traits and is incapable of promoting effective reform is an important and so far relatively untouched bulkhead of support for the institutional theory. While the vessel may have foundered on the empirical shoals, it remains afloat. The purpose of this chapter is to test empirically the hypotheses dealing with reform.

Research and Reform

Chubb and Moe argue that the existing education system is incapable of making effective reforms. As evidence they point to the response of the system to a series of critical reports on the state of education (especially National Commission on Excellence in Education 1983). The response to these analyses was not to ignore, but enthusiastically to pursue efforts to correct the perceived problems. Chubb and Moe (1990, 10) say that in the 1980s, "the pace of change was frenetic. State after state adopted some permutation of a laundry list of reforms that, in the course of public study and debate, had come to be associated with effective education." Chubb and Moe (1990, 10–11) dismiss these efforts as failures.

Their dismissal seems somewhat premature. The empirical evidence they use to support their conclusions on performance is drawn from a data set based in the early 1980s, before many of the "ineffective" reforms had actually taken place.[1] In fact, little comprehensive attention has focused on how these reforms actually affected education performance, and providing such an examination is one of the goals of this chapter.

Chubb and Moe do not argue that the system will resist all reform, just certain *kinds* of reform. The controlling institutions will make any number of efforts to improve the end product, but not the one that will make a real difference—the controlling institutions will not face up to the possibility that they are the problem (Chubb and Moe 1990, 11). Nonetheless, based in no small part on Chubb and Moe's research, the controlling institutions have shown themselves quite willing to loosen their grasp on public education. For example, thirteen states have enacted some form of choice-based legislation (Carnegie Foundation 1992).

Many more states were quite aggressive in pursing the "laundry lists" of reform held to be ineffective by Chubb and Moe. The publication of the National Commission on Excellence in Education's *A Nation at Risk* in 1983 heralded a broad-based effort by state governments to improve their education systems. This so-called top-down reform came from state-level policymakers who viewed the poor performance of schools as a function of the quality of personnel within the education system and the methods available to them. The solutions were state mandates establishing new systemwide standards for both educator and student (Murphy 1990). The policy strategies adopted varied a good deal, making the states an excellent laboratory for comparative analysis. Many of these reforms were indeed held to be ineffective and not just by school choice advocates. A common element of reform was increased expenditures. This despite the fact that boosting teacher salaries and per pupil spending have repeatedly been dismissed as ineffective methods of improving performance (for extensive reviews of this literature, see Hanushek 1981, 1986).

Considerable descriptive analysis on the reforms of the 1980s exists, but little systematic empirical work, mainly owing to the difficulty in establishing causal linkages between state reforms and student performance (see National Center for Education Statistics 1992b). This chapter empirically examines the effects of top-down reform to see whether state-level policy efforts have achieved the goal of improving state-level educational outcomes. The institutional theory argues that reforms enacted by the existing institutions are little more than window dressing and will not work. If such reforms are demonstrably effective, it would undermine the case for school choice by showing the system is capable of improvement without radical change.

Finding the Causal Links

As noted earlier, a major reason for the inability of social science to provide concrete answers on state-level policy effects is the difficulty in establishing causal linkages between reforms and outcomes. A critical reason for this is the research perspective adopted by much of the literature. Much research has failed to pay sufficient attention to the unit of analysis. Most often, individual-level data have been used to criticize the larger education system (e.g., Chubb and Moe 1990). This raises all the problems inherent in using data collected at one level to infer relationships at another level. The need to adhere to the stated goal of comparing system-level measures is critical in an analysis of the states.

Top-down reforms may be mislabeled to some extent. State-level reforms were aimed at promoting broad-based improvements, that is, increasing performance systemwide (National Governors' Association 1986). The causal linkages become easier to sort out once the unit of analysis is clearly established. Because state reform was aimed at improving performance at a system level, the causal link of interest is between state reforms and state-level performance. Clearly the causal path sought by policymakers at this level is between *state* reforms and performance of the *state* education system as a whole. Thus the reforms are not seen as directed from the state to the individual student or a particular school or school district, but from the state to the performance of the entire state education system. This focuses the unit of analysis at the macro level—an important criterion established for this research—and avoids the complications inherent in making the micro-macro leap. The empirical proposition thus meets the established goal of examining the relationship between reforms and variation in system-level performance.

If the reforms were successful in making the causal connection at the macro level, then there should be observable relationships between state-level reforms and the outputs of the state-level education system. The unit of analysis is thus the states, and all data were measured and collected at the system level. Such aggregation will fail to account for the variation and impact of individual schools and school districts. The aim here is to ferret out the effects of state-level policies on state-level outcomes, so this is not considered a major drawback.

This assumes, of course, that school districts will implement these state reforms. The amount of state control over school districts varies dramatically by state, and the implementation literature suggests that many policy reforms will not be implemented or will be implemented in an unintended manner by the implementing agency (see Mazmanian and Sabatier 1989). In some instances this is not a problem because state agencies implemented the programs themselves (e.g., teacher competency tests). For other programs there is evidence that states have a number of options to enforce compliance and that many state reforms were carried out at the district level (Weiss 1990).

The problem of resisting reform policies at the district level is greatly diminished if viewed from a school choice perspective. Choice advocates see public education as a highly centralized, hierarchical system designed so that schools are forced to carry out the goals of the democratic bodies and bureaucracies that form that hierarchy, even if the schools disagree with the goals (Peterson 1990; Chubb and Moe 1990). This common perspective in the school choice literature obviously perceives a clear causal link between policy adoption at the state level and policy implementation at the school level.

While research based on school choice, principal-agent, and litigation models (Chubb and Moe 1990; McCubbins, Noll, and Weingast 1987; Wise 1979; Weiss 1990) has provided considerable evidence of the link between state-level policy adoption and local compliance, schools may not always follow the wishes of state government. At a minimum, however, strong anecdotal evidence suggests that when states make a commitment to education reforms, they can ensure a high level of local compliance and in doing so affect state-level education outputs (Chira 1993; Celis 1993). Although the reported impact of these reforms is mixed, empirical evidence of the macro link between state-level policy reform and a state's education system as a whole does exist. The goal now is to test the effects of this relationship.

The Dependent Variable

In order to proceed, the first critical step is to construct an acceptable measure of education performance at the state level. Measuring the performance of state education systems is an area of some controversy and varied estimation. The favored yardstick of system-level education performance has been an aggregated measure of standardized tests, usually the SAT or American College Testing Program (ACT) (Morgan and Watson 1987; Lehnen 1992). Graduation-rate measures have also been used, but are considered an inferior measure. Graduation-rate data are often severely dated and, more important, are not considered an equivalent yardstick. Because the quality of schools varies greatly from state to state, high school diplomas are not reliable indicators of academic achievement. While high graduation rates may be the product of superior education policies, they may also be the product of inferior and ill-enforced standards. Such flaws make graduation rates a poor choice for a measure to help identify effective policies.

Measures based on standardized tests have also been widely and justifiably criticized. The favored alternative has been to measure student performance on the same cohort of students at two different times and to take the improvement in scores, or some derivation thereof, as the dependent variable (variously called value-added or gain indicators). Proponents argue that this measure is superior because it better captures the impact of the education system while controlling for background characteristics such as raw cognitive ability and family socioeconomic status (see Hanushek and Taylor 1990; Meyer 1992).

Such arguments make a great deal of sense. Unfortunately, what such measures gain in accuracy, they lose in practicality.[2] While data sets exist that offer such possibilities, they are limited both in number and in the time periods available for study.[3] The prohibitive expense of collecting such data simply does not make such a measure a realistic alternative in many cases.

This study uses ACT and SAT scores as the preferred alternative. Although the tests were not designed as measures of performance, in the absence of any real alternative this is exactly how state policymakers have used them (Lehnen 1992). Scores on the SAT and ACT are what policymakers commonly use as a judgment criterion for state education systems, so it seems reasonable to assume such a measure should capture the intended effects, if any, of reform policies. Using this measure, however, creates three main difficulties that must be addressed before the study can proceed. First, comparisons among state averages may be misleading because such scores do not take into account the number of students taking the examination. The smaller the percentage of the student population taking the test, the higher the mean score tends to be. Powell and Steelman (1984) reported that almost three-fourths of the variation in state SAT scores could be attributed to the percentage of students taking the test.

This criticism is the most easily countered. The U.S. Department of Education (DOE) solves this problem by setting a minimum of 31.5 percent of those eligible actually taking the test before reporting a state's mean score on its "wall charts." The bivariate correlation between the complete sample of 1982 SAT scores (used by Powell and Steelman) and the percentage of students taking the test is .857. Using the DOE 31.5 percent minimum, the linear relationship disappears; the resulting correlation is .001.

The DOE "solution" creates its own problem and raises a second criticism of using SAT and ACT scores. The results reported by the DOE consist of two truncated samples: SAT-dominant states (minimum of 31.5 percent students taking SAT) and ACT-dominant states (minimum of 31.5 percent students taking ACT). To get a measure applicable to all fifty states, the SAT and ACT scores must be standardized to permit the two DOE state samples to be merged.

Extrapolating a common and comparable score from two different tests has been a much debated subject. Scholars have generally assumed the SAT and ACT are compatible enough to transform the scores into a single indicator of state-level education performance (see Astin 1971; Wainer 1986; Lehnen 1992). But the methods of accomplishing this have been far from uniform. They have ranged from relatively simple arithmetic formulas such as the Wainer Transformation (Wainer 1986) to more complex statistical manipulations that attempt to control for such problems as combining data pools with differing means and standard deviations (for a good review of this literature and the various methods proposed, see Lehnen 1992).

The transformation here employs the maxim that simpler is better. A standardized education index (SEI) is constructed using a state's mean SAT or ACT score expressed as a percentage of the highest score possible. On a national level, and where reasonable dual state scores exist, these percentages have fluctuated in unison during the past two decades, with ACT means consistently running about 5 percentage points below SAT means. To account for this difference, 5 points are added to the ACT percentages; the two state samples are then merged.[4] Although quite a simple operation, it is not dissimilar from other proposed transformations[5] and appears to capture the SAT and ACT scores quite well. The bivariate correlation between the SEI and state SAT scores is .997, and between the SEI and state ACT scores, .999.

The third criticism aimed at indexes constructed from SAT and ACT scores is that no amount of statistical manipulation can overcome their nonrandom nature. This is not simply a question of sample size. Students taking these tests are a highly self-selecting group—specifically, those intending to attend college. Generalizing from this sample to the target population may be attacked as invalid. Countering such arguments is empirical evidence that indexes such as the SEI are valid measures of the underlying concepts. For example, the SEI's external validity is bolstered by its strong association with the U.S. Department of Education's experimental 1990 eighth-grade math exam ($r = .77$).[6] It is also strongly associated with the percentage of a state's population that has graduated from high school ($r = .68$).

Research Design

The goal of this research is to construct a model of state-level education outcomes capable of testing the utility of state education policies. Building a single model that encompasses the major elements of previous research is a difficult if not impossible task. Dozens of variables and measurements have been incorporated into empirical analyses with sometimes differing results. Controlling for sources of variation other than policy is thus a major challenge to model specification.

To meet this challenge a single control variable is used—a lagged version of the dependent variable. This accomplishes two important goals. First, it sets a very high threshold for any other variable to attain statistical significance. Thus it increases confidence that inferred relationships actually exist. Second, and more important, it acts as a blanket control variable. While there is much variation in education outcomes among states, there is very little variation within them. Using the SEI—or any other given measure of education performance—it is immediately apparent that individual state scores are reasonably stable over time and that some states consistently score higher than others. It is thus logical to model state-level educational outcomes for any given year as a function of outcomes for previous years.

The source of interstate variation is the topic of much heated debate. Whether Minnesota produces higher SAT scores than, say, Alabama, because of regional socioeconomics or demographics, historical commitment to education, support from the political system, or something else is not yet resolved. Regardless, a lagged version of the dependent variable in essence controls for all these possible sources of nonspecified variation. Whatever the reasons for one state's high score and another's low score, they are efficiently captured by the lagged variable. Any variable that achieves statistical significance in the face of such a strong control can be reasonably inferred to have an effect on the dependent variable.[7]

To test the effect of policy, variables representing the most common state-level education reforms of the 1980s were included. New standards for educators and students were a basic element of these reforms (Murphy 1990). Accordingly, one variable was included to measure if a state required a comprehensive test of academic skills for high school graduation, and another was used to measure if a state required teacher certification.[8]

Other common top-down reforms included curriculum mandates and requirements for lengthier school careers. To account for these reforms, variables were included measuring the minimum number of course units required for a high school diploma and the required school starting age. Another reform ardently pursued by many educators at the state level was a mandate for smaller class sizes. To represent such efforts the teacher/pupil ratio within a state was used. According to critics, all these reforms should have no effect on education outcomes, especially in the presence of a control as strong as the lagged variable included in the model.

Although not considered reforms, two other structure variables have been included in the recent policy changes. A school-size variable—measured as a ratio of total state enrollment to number of schools—was included here as a measure of the institutional differences among state education systems. Some states simply have larger schools and school districts than others, and school size has long been examined as a potential influence on academic performance. Larger schools can take advantage of economies of scale and arrange the division of labor among teachers to promote a specialized curriculum (Daft and

Becker 1980; Friedkin and Necochea 1988). Smaller schools, in contrast, can be more attentive to individual student needs and promote a more teamlike atmosphere that is conducive to learning (Powell, Farrar, and Cohen 1985). Because school size is something that can to some extent be controlled by state policymakers through financial support for staff and new school construction, this variable was designed to examine whether smaller, close-knit learning environments promote superior education performance.

Finally, a measure of the centralization of state education systems was included. This consisted of a ratio of state to district bureaucrats. The larger this ratio, the more top-heavy the bureaucratic hierarchy within a state. Similar to school size, this is not really a measure of reform but is intended to be a yardstick of the institutional and organizational structure of state education systems. Chubb and Moe argue that centralized bureaucratic systems are bad for education because they limit school autonomy by enforcing the mandates of democratically controlled institutions. Thus the institutional theory predicts the relationship here should be negative.

As a final control, three models with different lags are used. Each model is applied to a 1988 data set inclusive of forty-nine states.[9] In each model a state's 1988 SEI score is the dependent variable. The lagged controls for the individual models are the 1986, 1984, and 1980 SEI scores.

Results

Our findings indicate that the top-down reforms did have the intended positive effect on state education outcomes (see appendix, Table A.14, p. 152). Indeed, all our models indicate that the education reforms of the 1980s were not just window dressing but were effective policies that boosted education performance.

Two of the most interesting findings are that graduation test requirements and teacher certification improve education performance. These were two of the most common reforms enacted by states, and their utility has been the subject of much debate and controversy. Our model estimates that implementing a student graduation test improves a state's SEI score by .82 over the eight-year time period and by lesser amounts over shorter time periods. The teacher certification policy is statistically significant and indicates an improvement of .26 in a state's

SEI score during the most recent two-year period studied; the modest delay in the impact of teacher certification in all likelihood results from the gradual influx of new teachers who were forced to meet these higher standards.

Although the gains attributed to these policies seem small, it should be kept in mind that state SEI scores have historically been extremely stable over time. A shift of even a point in a single year is considerable, so such gains should not be considered insignificant.[10] The reforms appear to have had a modest incremental effect that may become more apparent with the passage of time. The policy of seeking to improve overall performance by setting higher standards and expectations does appear to work.

The most consistent variable is that for number of students per school. States with smaller school sizes tend to have higher performance scores. For every additional student per school, our models estimate that SEI scores fall between .002 and .004 points. State education systems characterized by smaller, close-knit learning environments have higher levels of achievements. Institutional differences are thus seen as significant, and any advantages deriving from the economies of scale gained by larger schools are offset by losses in performance.

Teacher/pupil ratios were significant in two of the three models.[11] The positive, significant relationships indicate that students perform better in larger classes. Although this appears counterintuitive, part of the explanation is the limited range of the data at the state level. Education scholars advocating smaller classes feel that marginal reductions have little impact; only major reductions will generate real improvements. The positive relationship, therefore, likely reflects other factors that were not included in the model. The most likely omitted variable that would explain this relationship is motivation. That is, school systems with high student-to-teacher ratios may well have felt greater pressure to act during the 1980s reform era. If such systems did adopt more policies—and the preliminary analyses suggest that they did—the teacher/pupil ratio measure may be capturing the effects of reform efforts we were unable to measure.[12]

Two of the policy variables, those dealing with compulsory school starting ages and the number of units required for a high school diploma, failed to achieve statistical significance in any model. The starting-age variable, in particular, displays a coefficient that stays fairly stable around zero, which is strong evidence that this particular policy has little payoff. The curriculum variable is stable across the three models and hovers just below the acceptable thresholds of statistical significance. Although the coefficient's insignificance prevents making any supportable inference, it appears the big problem here may be a relatively small number of cases—which reduces the likelihood of achieving statistical significance—rather than an ineffective policy. As other variables indicate that setting high expectations helps to improve performance, we are unwilling to dismiss strong curriculum requirements as ineffective.

The centralization variable also failed to achieve statistical significance in any model. Not only was the variable insignificant, but its slope was positive in all three models. This finding runs counter to the expectations of the institutional theory, which predicts that centralized systems are ineffectively organized and promote lower performance outputs. Our findings indicate that, contrary to the school choice perspective, more centralized state systems record higher levels of education performance. This may result from a centralized system's greater ability to set and enforce high standards.

As expected, the lagged control variable was highly significant and accounted for the lion's share of the variance in all three models. Also unsurprising is that the shorter the lag, the stronger the control variable. This explains why the impact of the other variables tends to get smaller as the control variable gets stronger. What is important is not the control variable's dominant role but the significant effects of the other variables in the presence of such an effective control.

Discussion and Conclusion

Our research presents evidence that the reforms of the 1980s did affect state-level education performance. Graduation tests, teacher certification, and smaller schools all showed positive and significant relationships with performance. The consistent performance of the course-requirement variable, although falling just short of acceptable statistical significance thresholds, also suggests that curriculum mandates may positively influence performance. Significantly, these effects were detectable in the presence of a highly dominant control variable designed to account for all nonspecified sources of variation.

These findings contradict the expectations of the institutional theory. The reforms enacted by the existing education system are not the mere window dressing of symbolic politics, but substantive contributions to improving education. The variation in performance among state education systems has been shown to be at least partly a function of the mix of policies that run them. In addition, the degree to which state education systems have centralized bureaucracies does not appear to be a factor in depressing performance, as predicted by the institutional theory. Not only was the variable aimed at capturing this concept insignificant, it was positively associated with performance in all three models. Centralization does not seem to be the villain school choice advocates portray.

Once again, the organizational focus of the institutional theory has not survived the empirical test. Contrary to the claims of school choice advocates, the controlling institutions of education seem to be making successful attempts to improve performance. The gains are not dramatic, and they certainly stop short of being a cure-all. Nonetheless, the reforms appear to be working.

Notes

1. Chubb and Moe's analyses are based on the High School and Beyond Sophomore Cohort First Followup (assembled in 1982), which used students who were sophomores in 1980 and seniors in 1982, and the High School and Beyond Administrator and Teacher Survey, assembled in 1984. They acknowledge the problems of using dated material to make contemporary generalizations (Chubb and Moe 1990, 232–33). They argue there is no bias in treating the analysis as contemporary, however, because both high- and low-achievement schools adopted organizational changes at roughly the same rate (reported in Chubb and Moe 1990, Table A-1). Given the sweeping changes made throughout the 1980s—Chubb and Moe's data stop at 1984—and the time lag that can reasonably be expected between introduction of reform and effect, this argument seems questionable. For example, it is unrealistic to adopt a teacher certification program and expect high school seniors' SAT scores to increase immediately. Reform successes are incremental over time, not immediate.

2. Even the claims of accuracy of such measures are open to criticism. At the individual level, subtracting two scores that contain some measurement error compounds the total error in relation to the variation that taps the underlying concept. Standardized tests clearly contain some measurement error. In many instances the change in scores may be so small (Chubb and Moe's scores average two test questions) that measurement error may well dwarf any real variation.

3. The High School and Beyond data set employed by Chubb and Moe, and many other researchers, is one such possibility. The big problem here is that much of the data was collected before the wave of top-down reforms was enacted. Obviously, this makes that data set inappropriate for this research.

4. This results in merging an ACT sample with a mean of 57.2 and a standard deviation of 2.7, and an SAT sample with a mean of 55.7 and a standard deviation of 1.6.

5. The Wainer Transformation, for example, turns ACT scores into estimated SAT scores by the following formula: $W = 110 + 40A$, where W is the estimated SAT score, and A is the state average ACT score.

6. This measure avoids the selection bias of the SAT and ACT and is available for thirty-seven of the fifty states.

7. A number of statistical tests were conducted to provide empirical support for the argument that the lagged control performed as argued. A second model was constructed to include four fiscal and socioeconomic controls: average teacher salary, teenage birthrates, percentage of population living in urban areas, and per pupil expenditures. A joint F-test between the two models resulted in an F of 0.78. The controls made absolutely no difference to the model.

In addition, two separate models were constructed, one for fiscal impacts and one for socioeconomic impacts. These consisted of the lagged control variable and a list of potential school expenditure and socioeconomic controls. Not a single variable besides the control was statistically significant.

As a final test, theory was abandoned and all policy, socioeconomic, and fiscal variables were submitted to a step-wise procedure. Not a single socioeconomic or fiscal variable was picked up.

The conclusion of this series of tests is that the lagged control variable is acting as described. Although several of the fiscal and socioeconomic controls have strong relationships with the dependent variable, these completely disappear in the presence of the lagged control. The lagged control functions well in its role of capturing all potential sources of nonspecified variation.

8. Unless otherwise noted, the source for all variables is the *Overview and Inventory of State Requirements for School Coursework and Attendance* or *Education Digest*.

Selecting the policy variables to be included in our model proved to be a major challenge. Including the contents of all the "laundry lists" used by all states would have created a daunting—and statistically problematical—challenge. The policy variables we selected are thus those that have been identified by previous studies as the most common state-level education reforms of the 1980s (National Center for Education Statistics 1992b; Murphy 1990).

9. Washington State did not report ACT or SAT scores to the Department of Education for the period studied and is therefore excluded. The only other state with missing data, and which is therefore excluded from some models, was Texas.

10. As noted in note 10 of the previous chapter, the coefficient reflects the increase for one year but that increase continues to affect the dependent variable by working though the lagged dependent variable. For example, the total impact of the coefficient found in the four-year lag for the graduation test is 3.26 points assuming the patterns continue. In the long run, these coefficients can have a major impact on performance.

11. This variable was logged to correct for skewness in the data, so substantive interpretation of the coefficients is difficult.

12. Measuring highly subjective concepts such as motivation and pressure is, needless to say, very difficult.

———— Seven ————

Fixin' What Ain't Broke: Education Performance in the 1980s

The institutional theory supporting school choice now appears to be in danger of collapsing from the weight of the empirical evidence stacked against it. All six of the hypotheses drawn from Chubb and Moe's reasoning (see Table 3.1, p. 42) have failed the empirical test at both district and state levels. But the institutional theory still has at least two remaining lines of defense.

One is that there is no comprehensive, national-level test of its hypotheses across time as well as space. The research in chapter six provides preliminary evidence that the top-down reforms of the 1980s worked, but the model is something of a blunt instrument. Its cross-sectional nature captured the differences among states, but deliberately ignored the possibility of variation within states. The reforms of the 1980s were not simply adopted to improve, say, Alabama's performance relative to California's. Policymakers sought to improve their own state's historical performance (see National Center for Education Statistics 1992b). The lagged variables included in the previous chapter's model effectively controlled for such temporal effects, but did little to explain them. The potential effects of changes within states during the reform period were, in essence, removed from the analysis. School choice advocates might argue that, within states, reforms had no real impact, and in ignoring this temporal source of variation the research misses support for the institutional theory.[1]

The second and perhaps most important remaining defense for the institutional theory is that there has been no direct test of school choice. While the relationships posited by school choice advocates for the existing education system have failed to materialize, the efficiencies of the abstract education market continue to provide their theoretical benefits. As long as the education market remains largely nonexistent, school choice will remain a theoretical success.

By the early 1990s the ability of school choice theory to retreat into the abstract was becoming more constrained. Thirteen states adopted some form of choice legislation (see Carnegie Foundation 1992). Such programs vary greatly from state to state. Some states allow schools or school districts the option of pursuing choice programs, while others mandate a statewide open-enrollment policy. The actual movement of students from school to school is usually restricted by space requirements and explicit or implicit prohibitions against recruiting.[2] Still, the school choice reform movement has had enough adoptions that it is possible in a few places to see the embryonic beginnings of an education market. The relative novelty and paucity of such systems and the considerable differences among them mean that collecting comparative data is difficult. But the fact that they exist at all offers an opportunity for at least a preliminary, direct test of school choice claims.

The purpose of this chapter is to provide a comprehensive test of the American education system across time and space. Our research is designed to assess how the reforms of the 1980s—up to and including the adoption of limited statewide public choice—affected education outputs, and what roles internal institutional arrangements and external pressures played in the success or failure of such reforms.

The Causes of Macro-Level Education Performance

Existing research suggests the determinants of macro-level education performance can be classified into four broad categories: Internal controllable, external controllable, internal noncontrollable, and external noncontrollable. These categories are diagrammed and their components listed in Table 7.1.

The ability of education policymakers to affect education outputs is limited to the internal controllable cell. This cell lists the causes of macro-level performance identified by previous research that are internal to the education system and controllable by education policymakers. They include the institutional arrangements of the system (Brown 1992; Chubb and Moe 1988, 1990; Peterson 1990; Witte 1990), and the policies and reforms established and enforced by this organizational structure (Smith 1994; Murphy 1990; Bryk, Lee, and Smith 1990; Best 1993; Bowe, Ball, and Gold 1992).

Few of the external influences on the education system are controllable by education policymakers. The very top of the education hierar-

Table 7.1

Determinants of Macro-Level Education Performance

	Internal to education system	External to education system
Controllable by policymakers	Institutional/organizational arrangements	Democratic values
	Policy/reforms	
Noncontrollable by policymakers	Innate cognitive capacities of students	Social conditions/attitudes
	Historical performance	

chy—that is, governors and legislatures—can be included as internal components of the education system because Chubb and Moe (1990, 38–41) suggest that they somehow control the democratic values that run education. These policymakers are responsible for taking the values and demands of external constituencies and forcing them on education. This notion is reflected as a separate category in Table 7.1, but reality is not quite so clear-cut. What exactly constitutes an "external constituency" has never really been defined by Chubb and Moe or any other school choice research. A religion-based ideological coalition seeking the mandated inclusion of scientific creationism in the public school curriculum is clearly external to the education system. But what about teachers' unions? A key source of seemingly "external" values—that is, goals that block the demands of students and parents (Chubb and Moe 1990, 153–54)—it seems unrealistic to label any group consisting primarily of teachers as anything but internal. The "democratic values" lumped into the controllable-external category is thus deliberately vague. While the institutional theory strongly suggests some external causes of education performance are controllable by policymakers, it never clearly separates the internal and external characteristics of the system.

The noncontrollable categories are much easier to define. Internally, historical performance is the overriding factor influencing macro-level performance at the state level (see chapter six). Obviously, policymakers cannot change the past. There are also a host of social conditions and attitudes linked to education performance (Kozol 1991). For the most part these represent external pressures on the education system over which policymakers have at best only limited control. The problems of teenage pregnancy, drug use, crime, violence, and the disintegration of the inner-city family clearly influence education. Problems also stem from societal forces outside the education system. While education policymakers can and do make attempts to deal with such problems, to suggest they could control them is absurd.

Identifying the likely causes of macro-level education performance provides the first building block for a comprehensive test of the national education system. If the noncontrollable causes are held constant, the institutional theory posits predictable relationships for the internal controllable causes. These include a positive relationship between the adoption of school choice–based policies and education performance. With the causal categories of macro-level education performance identified, a model can now be constructed.

Theory

Controllable Causes

Of most immediate interest to education policymakers are factors causally related to performance that can be controlled. Internally, these can be divided into two broad categories: institutional arrangements and policy. The institutional theory argues that the former holds the key to improving education. According to Chubb and Moe (1988, 1990), the salient institutional features of the existing system are democratic control and bureaucracy. Substituting local autonomy and the freedom to choose for this institutional arrangement will improve education. Instead of taking their marching orders from the top—that is, from school boards and legislatures—schools will take their cues from the bottom, from the students and parents they serve. The decentralization of the controlling institutions will free the system to meet the demands from parents and students for quality education.

The institutional theory grants little credence to the policies stemming from the existing system. Until the institutional arrangements are changed, argue Chubb and Moe (1990, 10–11), reforms are destined for failure. If the institutional theory is correct, then democratic control and bureaucracy should be linked with decreased education outputs, and reform policies should have little impact on performance.

So far, little evidence has supported this perspective. Indeed, the findings of previous chapters point to exactly the opposite conclusion —that reform polices improve education and that democratic control and bureaucracy have, if anything, a positive effect on performance. A comprehensive test of the national education system can thus be predicated on two competing hypotheses dealing with controllable determinants of performance. The first is rooted in the institutional theory. This posits that states with institutional arrangements characterized by democratic control, centralization, and large bureaucracies should exhibit poorer macro-level performance than other states. Furthermore, the reform policies enacted by such states in the 1980s should show little relationship to performance because the real problem lies in the institutional arrangements.

The counterhypothesis is rooted in the empirical evidence of the previous chapters. This posits that the effects of institutional arrangements of state education systems will either be minimal or positive. The top-down reform policies will work by setting demands for higher standards (Murphy 1990). More centralized systems may be better suited to succeed because they have a greater ability to pass and enforce such uniform standards.

Noncontrollable Causes

In order to test the competing hypotheses dealing with the controllable determinants of performance, we must recognize and account for the noncontrollable causes. Most important is the historical performance of state education systems (see chapter six). The ranking among states on education performance measures changes little over time. Some states have always produced higher scores than others. Policymakers must recognize that they cannot alter history. Even the most reform-oriented state is not going to improve its rankings relative to other states in a short period of time.

While recognizing the importance of history, policymakers need not simply bow to an inevitable future. The task is to control for historical performance and then see what can work. Chapter six took some steps in this direction; but as a primarily cross-sectional analysis it did not account for within-state variation—the sort of variation most state policymakers are attempting to influence. To test the competing hypotheses on controllable education performance determinants adequately, we must control for historical rankings and then view variation across time and space. This will allow an analysis of what influences performance within and among states.

A more immediate concern of noncontrollable influence are prevailing social conditions and attitudes. Work such as Kozol's (1991) demonstrates convincingly that education cannot be held separate from external social pressures. Teenage pregnancies, drugs, violence, and many other problems that can contribute to poor performance cannot be blamed on the education system alone. A fair evaluation of the system's performance must reflect these outside influences.

Data and Methods

Pooled time-series analysis seems the most appropriate technique to meet the goals of this research. A pooled time series offers the advantage of analyzing effects across time and space (see Stimson 1985; Sayrs 1989). Cross-sectionally the focus of the study is the institutional arrangements of states, which (with some important exceptions) tend to be fairly stable across time. Longitudinally, the focus is the reform policies of the 1980s.

The dependent variable for the study is the SEI, the standardized education index score (based on SAT and ACT scores; see chapter six) for each state from 1981 to 1990, producing a pool that has fifty cross-sections and ten time points. With the dependent variable defined, and the cross-section and time parameters set, the critical task of specifying independent variables can begin.

Independent Variables

Controllable

Five variables were selected to test the hypotheses on reform. These included requirements for teacher certification, a mandatory test for high school graduation (measured as dummy variables), the number of pupils per teacher within the state system, a ratio of students to schools, and the financial resources devoted to education. All of these varied within states in the time period under study, and most have already been associated with education performance in cross-sectional studies (Smith and Meier 1993).

If the reform polices were effective, they should exhibit predictable relationships with the performance measure. Teacher certification and graduation test requirements were widely adopted by states. If setting higher standards did improve performance, within and across states, they should be positively related with the dependent variable. Smaller learning environments were also a widely pursued reform, and teacher/pupil ratios and students per school were included to measure these policy efforts. Finally, per capita expenditures were included to measure the relative resources that states devoted to education. To standardize this measure across time, it was converted to constant dollars.[3] The institutional theory posits that reforms without a fundamental change in institutional arrangements will be of limited value. If this perspective is correct, these variables should display at best weak relationships with education performance.

Three variables were included to test the hypotheses on institutional arrangements. The first was a dummy variable indicating an elected head of the state education system. The strongly antidemocratic perspective of the institutional theory predicts this variable should be negatively related to performance. More democracy means more constraints, as elected officials seek to serve the maxim of the electoral connection rather than the needs of parents and students. Conversely, previous evidence (see chapter four) indicates democratic control is beneficial to education. Democracy from this perspective is seen as an effective (though not necessarily efficient) means of meeting societal demands while providing some assurances that equity, although not guaranteed, will at least not be forgotten. If this is true, the relationship with performance should be positive, because systems with greater degrees of democratic control are better equipped to meet the broad demands of society.

The second institutional variable included was the number of a state's students in private schools, measured as a percentage of total enrollment. A key piece of evidence in the school choice argument is research showing that private schools do a better job of educating than their public school counterparts do (Coleman and Hoffer 1987; Coleman, Hoffer, and Kilgore 1982). This success is attributed to their freedom from democratic control and bureaucratic restraints (Chubb and Moe 1990, 67). Although enrollment in private schools is not really controllable by policymakers, it serves as an important institutional measure. From the perspective of the institutional theory, states with higher private school enrollments should have more students free from the institutional constraints of the public system. Private school enrollment, therefore, should be strongly and positively associated with performance. The counterhypothesis is that high private school enrollment is nothing more than a surrogate measure of relative wealth. This hypothesis also predicts a positive relationship, although a much weaker one when other controls are in place. The institutional theory predicts this variable to be a key indicator of state-level performance. The counterhypothesis predicts it to be a minor one.

The final institutional variable included in the model is the percentage of public employees involved in elementary and secondary education who are teachers.[4] This is designed to be a "tooth-to-tail" ratio, a yardstick of bureaucratization of a state's education system. The institutional theory posits the fewer teachers in a system and the more paper pushers, the lower the education performance. Previous evidence (see chapter four) indicates that more bureaucracy is associated with lower performance, but that it is the very issues bureaucracies are created to cope with—not bureaucracy itself—that are the problem. If the institutional theory is correct, there should be a strong, positive relationship between this variable and performance. Again, the counterhypothesis also predicts a positive relationship. Few would argue that putting more teachers in the system would lower education performance. Unlike the institutional theory, the counterhypothesis does not posit this to be a dominant predictor of performance.

The final controllable variable included in the model was school choice. This was measured as a dummy variable, with 1 indicating a state had adopted a blanket open-enrollment policy or had a statutory guarantee allowing students to attend the school of their choice.[5] All states in this category fall well short of the decentralized institutional arrangement envisioned by Chubb and Moe. No states have given up total control of education policy. Still, the fact that open enrollment exists is a significant policy development that in large part reflects the strength of the public choice movement. This should provide a preliminary gauge of the macro-level effectiveness of choice.

Noncontrollable

Three variables were included to account for performance determinants beyond the control of policymakers. The most important of these was historical performance. To account for the past performance of state education systems, each state's 1980 SEI was included as an independent variable. This was an attempt to isolate what really made a difference during the reform decade of the 1980s. The lagged SEI was designed to account for historical performance before 1980 (see chapter six). Any variance not explained by this variable must result from factors that occurred after 1980. If the model is correctly specified, these factors should be explained by the other variables included in the model.

Teen birthrates were included to measure the effects of external social pressures on education. Teen birthrates are strongly associated with poverty and other problems that could affect education (see Kozol 1991). The expected relationship is negative. Finally, a trend variable was included, measured as the year associated with each time point. This was included to capture any broad trend in education performance not reflected in the other variables over the time period studied. A negative trend variable would indicate that the national education system as a whole shows a general decay in performance. Such a finding would bolster the institutional theory, which a priori assumes the system is failing. A positive trend variable would indicate that the system is improving. Obviously this would raise questions about the a priori assumption of the problem that choice is designed to fix.[6]

Results

The results of the analysis show strong evidence that the institutional theory is a poor explanation of macro-level education performance (see appendix, Table A.15, p. 153). In virtually every area, the relationships predicted by the institutional theory fail to appear.

Most important for the institutional theory is the complete failure of the school choice indicator. Statewide open-enrollment programs are associated with a *decrease* in education performance. All things held constant, an embryonic public choice program actually has exactly the opposite effect of that intended. The coefficient estimates that states adopting open enrollment saw their SEI scores drop by almost a full point (.86). This finding is a serious challenge to school choice. Although this variable measures only a small fraction of the full-blown choice model advocated by Chubb and Moe, it is nonetheless strong empirical evidence that choice will not live up to expectations.[7]

The reform policies of the 1980s appear to work across time as well as space. All other things being equal, a teacher certification program was worth a .23 increase in the SEI, and a mandatory graduation test, .59. These two policies thus combine to raise a state's SEI score almost a full point. Given the highly stable nature of the SEI across time, this is a significant gain. Once again, the results indicate smaller learning environments are conducive to better performance. The coefficient for students per school shows larger schools are negatively associated with performance.[8] Unlike the results reported in the cross-sectional analysis of chapter six, teacher/pupil ratios are also negatively associated with performance. By adding the time dimension, it appears that class size makes a difference. As states successfully sought to reduce class size, they also increased education performance.

The single reform policy that did not perform as policymakers intended was the diversion of more resources into education. The spending variable is negatively related to performance, although the coefficient is close to zero and may actually reflect a nonrelationship. Such a finding would support much existing research (see Hanushek 1981, 1986), but the negative slope may mean the relationship is more complicated than simply saying money has no effect. The states that increased their educational spending the most during the 1980s tended to be states with historically low performance. Expenditures outstripped any performance gains—hence the negative slope—but may have been necessary to support other reforms, such as smaller class sizes, that did have positive impacts.

The institutional variables also failed to live up to the expectations of the institutional theory. An elected education head is associated with approximately a .4 increase in the SEI. This strong, positive relationship is the exact opposite of that predicted by the institutional theory and provides more evidence that democracy is not bad for education. Private school enrollment is positively related to performance, but the coefficient is virtually indistinguishable from zero. If we treat the slope as different from zero, it estimates that 50 percent of a state's enrollment would have to be in private schools to raise the SEI by a single point. This hardly supports a perspective that private schools are vastly superior at educating students.

The single variable offering some measure of comfort to the institutional theory is the tooth-to-tail staff ratio. The positive slope indicates that more teachers—and consequently fewer bureaucrats—mean higher performance, but the estimated impact of the variable is small. A 1 percentage point increase in the number of teachers is associated with a .02 increase in the SEI—meaning an increase of 50 percentage points is required to move the SEI a full point. Still, even the most hardened bureaucrat would hesitate to argue that fewer teachers and more bureaucrats constitute a better way to educate students. The impression here is that the effect of institutional arrangements that are bureaucratically top-heavy is detectable, but a far cry from the primary determinant of performance portrayed by the institutional theory. Because bureaucracy may well be a surrogate variable for external pressures on the system (see chapter four), and states with strongly centralized bureaucracies seem to be beneficial to education (see chapter six), even the mild negative relationship reported here is questionable.

As expected, teen birthrates were negatively associated with performance, although perhaps not as strongly as one would expect. The coefficient estimates an increase of 100 births per 1,000 women aged 15–19 is associated with a decrease of .01 in the SEI. External pressure is exerting some influence on education performance, but it does not appear to be overwhelming.

The most dominant variable in the model is the lagged SEI measure. This indicates policymakers should be conscious of the past performance of the system. No amount of reform is likely to trigger radical gains. For the states that are comparatively poor performers, even significant gains—increases of a point or two—are unlikely to alter their rank with other states. In some instances policymakers are faced with a century or more of official neglect. Change in the cumulative effects of such official disinterest in education is unlikely to occur in a year, or even a decade. Although the cure-all promises of public choice argue such results can be achieved, it is more realistic to seek incremental gains.

The trend variable indicates that this is exactly what happened during the 1980s. Holding all other variables constant, this coefficient indicates that SEI scores increased by .09 per year throughout the 1980s. No large gains, but certainly no losses. The gradual upward trend in SEI scores indicates that the education system made some modest upward gains during the past decade.[9] This finding stands in direct contrast to the descriptions of a system spiraling into decay.

Conclusion

This chapter provided a comprehensive test of the macro-level education system in the United States during the 1980s. The results indicate that the institutional theory is a poor explanatory model. The institutional arrangements the theory posits to be key factors in performance are not shown in the results or are in the opposite directions predicted. Embryonic school choice programs are not associated with any gains in performance—they are, in fact, associated with a loss. The reforms that school choice theorists argued to be the ineffective distractions of symbolic politics are instead associated with solid and significant gains in performance. A system portrayed in steady decline instead seems to be improving. The virtual uniform failure of the institutional theory in this test raises serious questions about its utility as an explanation of education and as an aid to public policymaking. Cut off from its traditional abstract maneuvering room, the institutional theory appears to be incapable of defending school choice on the empirical battlefield.

Notes

1. This is of no small concern. As observed in chapter six, there is little variation within states. If reforms are not associated with this intrastate variation, critics could argue that these policies failed their primary mission—to raise the individual state's education outputs.

2. Minnesota is regarded as the pioneer of statewide choice. It has a long history of pursuing innovative education programs and phased in a statewide open-enrollment policy—allowing students to choose any school—in 1987.

3. All data were collected from various years of *The Digest of Education Statistics* and *The Statistical Abstract of the United States*. Not all data were available for all years in all states. Because a pooled time series is sensitive to such gaps, missing data were estimated by taking the mean of the two closest time points of the same measure in the same state. Because most of the missing data dealt with one or two gaps on variables with little within-state variation (data were available for all years for all the policy variables), this is unlikely to produce any serious bias in the analysis.

The only variable with large gaps that needed to be filled in was for private school enrollment. Only two observations were available for this variable for the time period studied: 1980 and 1989. The 1980 data were used for 1981, and the 1989 data were used for 1989 and 1990. The rest of the years were interpolated using these two time points. For most states, the percentage of total enrollment in private schools appeared to be fairly stable, and the means are thus considered reliable estimates.

The only other estimation required was for the SEI of Washington State, which did not report SAT or ACT scores to the Department of Education for the time period studied. The scores included were based on state SAT scores reported from the early 1980s. These scores did not meet the DOE criterion of including 30.5 percent of those eligible actually taking the test (the actual figure was 19 percent; see Powell and Steelman 1984). The scores, however, were very close to estimates generated by a series of regression model similar to that presented in chapter six.

4. The centralization variable used in chapter six was not a realistic option because of lack of data.

5. The information for this variable was taken from the descriptions of legislative school choice activity reported by the Carnegie Foundation (1992).

6. The resulting model is specified thus:

$$SEI = b_1NTE + b_2GRADTEST + b_3TEACHRAT + b_4SDTS + b_5PERCAP + b_6CHOICE + b_7PVENROL + b_8ELECT + b_9STAFF + b_{10}TBIR + b_{11}YEAR + b_{12}SEI80$$

Where:

SEI	=	standardized education index, calculated for each year for each state.
NTE	=	a dummy variable, with 1 indicating that a state required teacher certification through the National Teacher Examination.
GRADTEST	=	a dummy variable, with 1 indicating a required test for high school graduation.
TEACHRAT	=	a ratio of the number of students per teacher within a state's elementary and secondary education system.
SDTS	=	the mean number of students per school within a state.
PERCAP	=	per pupil expenditures in constant (1987) dollars, expressed as a percentage of per capita income (constant 1982 dollars) within a state.
CHOICE	=	a dummy variable, with 1 indicating a statewide open-enrollment or choice policy.
PVENROL	=	total private school enrollment, measured as a percentage of total public school enrollment.
ELECT	=	a dummy variable, with 1 indicating an elected head of the state education system.
STAFF	=	percentage of total employees in public elementary and secondary education who are teachers.
TBIR	=	number of teen pregnancies per 1,000 women aged 15–19.
YEAR	=	a countervariable measured as the year the other observations in the cross-section were taken.
SEI80	=	a state's 1980 SEI score. This measure was a constant across time.

Per pupil expenditures were measured in constant dollars to standardize the measure across time. These figures were expressed as a percentage of per capita income within states to standardize the measure across space.

This model was applied to a pooled data set of all fifty states from 1981 to 1990. Pooled designs often require some statistical manipulation to overcome the methodological challenges inherent in the technique (see Stimson 1985; Sayrs 1989). This model was no exception. Initial diagnostics indicated heteroskedasticity was at acceptable levels, but there was substantial contamination from autocorrelation (estimated Rho of .58). To address this problem, the model was reestimated using a generalized least-squares error components model. This successfully removed the autocorrelation problem, and the GLS coefficients are reported.

There are four basic approaches to a pooled time-series analysis—OLS, least squares with dummy variables, GLS error components, and GLS-ARMA (see Stimson 1985). All four techniques were used to estimate the model. The model proved to be quite robust, with coefficients staying quite stable across techniques. Diagnostics show the reported model includes some unaccounted for heteroskedasticity from unit effects. But neither the fullblown LSDV model nor a reduced model with dummies for the significant cross-sections appreciably altered the results. As dummies for cross-sections are essentially measures of "ignorance" (Stimson 1985)—that is, they account for disturbances but do nothing to explain them—and in the interests of parsimony, the more compact GLS error components model is reported.

7. The negative slope of the public choice variable is almost certainly not caused by a skewed distribution in which only poorly performing states adopted open enrollment. Indeed, the earliest open-enrollment program was adopted by Minnesota in 1987, and this state was therefore most closely associated with macro-level choice. Minnesota consistently has among the highest SEI scores in the nation.

8. The table shows this to be a statistically insignificant variable. The *t*-scores are included as a standard reporting procedure, but it should be realized that in this case they are of limited use. Given the defined parameters—state education systems in the 1980s—this data set constitutes a *population* and not a *sample*.

9. This estimate fits quite well with the raw data. The coefficient indicates SEI scores should have risen by just under a point during the 1980s. The mean SEI in 1980 was 55.7, in 1990 it was 56.4. The standard deviations associated with these means decreased, from 3 in 1980 to 2.5 in 1990.

——— Eight ———

Choice across the Borders

A common catalyst behind reform movements such as school choice is the belief that America's education system is inferior to the systems of its economic competitors. Reports of a disintegrating education infrastructure invoke images of a nation prostrate before its high-tech global competition and are a powerful normative argument for choice-based reforms. As Chubb and Moe (1990, 1) put it, "schools are failing in their core academic mission . . . so crucial to a future of sophisticated technology and international competition." Empirical analysis may rob school choice of its theoretical supports within the United States. But the bogeyman of foreign competition remains a staunch ally of school choice and is repeatedly pressed into its service.

Objectively examining the status of the American education system in a global context is difficult. Hardly a month goes by without new claims that U.S. students are academically backward. To take just one widely quoted example, the 1988 International Assessment of Educational Progress reported U.S. students to be global dunces in math and science at age thirteen.[1] Such reports are used as calls to action for reformers and are employed to pressure policymakers into supporting such efforts.

Such reports are misleading. Students in different countries are introduced to different concepts at different times. It is unclear whether measuring education achievement at age thirteen is more important than measuring achievement at age ten or eighteen or twenty-two. The later the achievement measure is taken, the stronger the United States finishes in international comparisons. For example, there are fewer high school dropouts and more twenty-two year olds with a bachelor's degree in the United States than in any other country in the world. Because the higher education system in this country has a reputation for high quality and attracts thousands of students from other countries, it seems somewhat contradictory to argue that a nation of secondary school dunces produces more college graduates than anyone else and then goes on to lead the world in the production of graduate degrees.

Indeed, some political scientists have repeatedly argued that the U.S. citizenry is the most educated in the world. Comparative voting behavior scholars have long held the American electorate to be better educated than its international counterparts. "Not only does the United States have the most educated citizenry," argues one scholar, "but education has much more direct impact on voter turnout" (Powell 1986).[2] The argument that the American education system is *superior* to its international counterparts has support from an impressive array of empirical studies. Unlike the reports of the failure of American education, evidence of a successful system is simply ignored (for a good review of this issue, see Bracey 1993).

Sorting out whether America is a country of academic underachievers or a nation of intellectually superior *uber*-voters is virtually impossible given the available data, or rather lack of data. No data available will support a sophisticated analysis aimed at resolving this paradox. The Sandia National Laboratories (1993) comprehensive report on education supports this view, saying that while rough comparisons are possible, "the major differences in education systems and cultures across countries" diminish their value.

Given the lack of firm evidence, what is available can be manipulated into a powerful normative argument. While school choice and other reform advocates are quick to play the global card, they are curiously slow to examine the education systems that threaten to leave America's behind.[3] Surely, if the education systems of our global competitors are producing better students, we should study and perhaps emulate their formula for success? The lack of data makes hard quantitative analysis impossible, but there is no reason not at least to make a descriptive analysis of successful systems and attempt some preliminary conclusions. Beginning with the premise that, as school choice advocates argue, institutional arrangements are causally related to education outputs, that is what this chapter proposes to do.

This chapter examines the education systems of the United Kingdom, Germany, and Japan. Germany and Japan were chosen because they are among America's strongest economic competitors. The United Kingdom, although also a forceful global competitor, was selected mainly owing to its cultural ties to the United States and because it has actually adopted a school choice system. The objective of the analysis is to describe in general terms the education system within each country and identify its primary institutional features, focusing on whether it has a centralized curriculum and a centralized bureaucracy governing education. As presented by Chubb and Moe, the institutional theory is a uniquely American explanation of education; however, the basic economic precepts it springs from can easily be applied in other countries. Indeed, the UK's adoption of a choice-based education system was based on virtually the same economic arguments mounted by Chubb and Moe (see Bowe, Ball, and Gold 1992). If such arguments are valid, then we should expect the "successful" education systems of America's global competitors to be market based.

Germany

Compared to American schools, European schools are much more centralized and much more elitist. They are characterized by centralized curricula and early "tracking" of students into academic or vocational career paths (Husen 1983). Vocational paths often end in apprenticeships without a high school diploma. Germany is no exception, even though it has one of the more decentralized systems on the Continent.

The organizational structure of the German education system is currently in a state of flux. The reunification of East and West Germany brought together two quite different approaches to education, and meshing the two into a compatible synthesis has raised a number of problems. Unlike many European countries, education in the old West Germany was not controlled by a centralized national bureaucracy. Education was and is a creature of federalism, with most of the authority for programs and curriculum content centered in the *Länder* (i.e., at state level).

The West German education structure is generally based on a tripartite system characterized by early tracking. Early selection in primary school leads to tracking into the *Gymnasium* (grammar school), *Realschule* (technical or intermediate school), and the *Hauptschule* (secondary modern). Education under the communist regime of East Germany was a more authoritarian and centralized affair. It was used as a tool for "ideological indoctrination" and was based on a much more comprehensive organizational structure ("Eastern Pendulum Swings Back" 1990).

With reunification, the power over education has for the most part been vested in state governments in eastern Germany, as it is in their western counterparts. In some sectors of the former East Germany there has been more enthusiasm for even greater decentralization of education powers, with a focus on providing autonomy for independent schools ("Eastern Pendulum Swings Back" 1990). Perhaps even more encouraging for school choice advocates in this country is an increasing tendency across all of Germany to view education in economic terms, with concerns being voiced about "cost efficiency" and "customer satisfaction" in schools. But in general, states in eastern Germany—with strong encouragement from western state governments—have adopted the tripartite system, and education remains firmly under the control of state governments.

This fragmentation results in marked differences in the characteristics of education within each state. These differences primarily spring from the political and ideological nature of the controlling state government. States controlled by Social Democrats tend to have more comprehensive systems, with tracking occurring later in the school career. The Christian Democratic/Social Christian states tend to place much more emphasis on achievement standards. Such differences have been widely noted by scholars and have resulted in something of a geographical split in the nature of education. The northern states, for example, are noted to have more liberal education systems than the utilitarian focus of southern Bavaria (McLean 1993). In short, education goals are not only controlled democratically in Germany but there are partisan differences in terms of these goals. Even accounting for such observable differences and the increasing attention to push autonomy downward, the German system is much more uniform than its American counterpart.

While there is no mandated national curriculum, there is virtually a de facto one. After thirty years of negotiation among state governments, the sixteen *Länder* of the old Federal Republic of Germany have achieved approximately 70 percent commonality. Although substantive areas of ideological and political disagreement remain among the state governments over education, the vast majority "still agree upon a very substantial area of common ground in curriculum and assessment" (McLean 1993). Similar types of uniformity are reasonably expected to appear in the states of eastern Germany. Certainly there is nothing comparable in the United States to the regular conferences of *Länder kultur* ministers, where issues in education are faced and cooperative agreements forged. Although among the most fragmented systems on the Continent, the German education system seems much more centralized and structured than the American.[4] Democratic control in the United States, a prime school choice concern, at least stops short of being an openly partisan issue with goals subject to change with electoral victories.

Viewed for its potential contribution to reform in the United States, the institutional features of the German system seem to come with a mixed bag of advantages and disadvantages. The tripartite system of early selection seems to provide good college preparatory tracks and, perhaps more important for the larger picture in the United States, excellent technical training for highly skilled labor. The *Realschule,* coupled with a proven apprenticeship program, results in many eighteen year olds in the job market having highly valued technical skills (Hamilton 1990). The big problem seems to be students who "fail to make the grade" and end up in the *Hauptschule.* As expressed by the *Times Educational Supplement* "Eastern Pendulum Swings Back" (1990, 14): "Nobody wants the *Hauptschule,* and for good reason: in the Federal Republic, it is now universally regarded as the 'left-overs school' and studies constantly confirm the growing difficulties in securing adequate training or employment."

Introducing greater institutionalized tracking into the U.S. education system would seem politically questionable at best. Universal access has been a cherished goal of American education at least since the beginnings of the desegregation movement. The sensitive issue of who would end up in America's *Hauptschule* is politically charged, and it hardly seems an exaggeration to suggest that many inner-city schools already serve the same purpose (Oakes 1985). Institutionalizing them as the "leftovers" would discredit any claims reformers made to equity.

Increasing centralization of education at the state level seems a more realistic option. Indeed, there has been movement toward this for more than a decade. Many of the reforms of the 1980s concentrated more responsibility for education at the state level. South Carolina, for example, passed its Education Improvement Act in 1984. This legislation raised sales taxes to fund a broad series of reforms including basic-skills tests and setting and enforcing higher academic standards (Chira 1993). Many other states increased their control over curriculum through mandated minimum course requirements (National Center for Education Statistics 1992b). Still, state governments have weak control over education compared to their German counterparts. They do not exercise anything like rigid control over curriculum. There is nothing comparable to the *kultur* minister in terms of prestige or power. A level of cooperation that would produce 70 percent commonality in curricula across the United States seems currently unrealistic.

Regardless of the political feasibility, the most striking institutional characteristics of the German system—early selection, tracking, and centralized democratic state control—are all unacceptable to the school choice argument. Indeed, school choice is the virtual opposite of the German system. Compared to Germany, the United States has a highly fragmented education system, with little uniformity and a high degree of local autonomy. To compete better with economic powerhouses such as Germany, school choice advocates are, in essence, arguing that increasing these differences will improve the failing American education system.

Japan

Even more than Germany, Japan is considered not just a competitor but an economic threat to the United States. If, as school choice advocates argue, education is the key to competitiveness in a high-tech world (see Chubb and Moe 1990, 1), it seems only logical to examine the education infrastructure that helped vault Japan's economy into global prominence.

Even a cursory examination quickly reveals why school choice advocates are reluctant to press comparisons with Japan beyond the dismal scores of American students in selective cross-national studies. Compared to Japan, even Germany has a highly decentralized system. The primary institutional feature of the Japanese education system is the Ministry of Education, "responsible for the uniform content and even distribution of educational resources across the population" (White 1987). Thus virtually every aspect of elementary and secondary education is controlled by a centralized bureaucracy. The ministry controls curricula, approves textbooks, and has a strong policy function, preparing budgets and other legislation for consideration by the Diet, the Japanese parliament.

Ironically, despite the centralization, the modern Japanese education system is actually based on the American model. Following the Occupation after World War II, local school boards, parent-teacher associations, and teachers' unions were formed across the country. Japanese society recognized that education was critical to building a modern industrialized economy, and there was a successful effort to centralize education at the national level (White 1987, 63–65). As in other cultural dimensions, in education the Japanese tend to stress the group rather than the individual.

A second defining characteristic of the Japanese system is the institutionalized high school entrance examination system. Within Japanese schools there is no tracking. But there is a highly competitive examination system that determines which high school a student will attend.[5] Because getting into the right high school is critical to future career success, the pressure to perform on these examinations is intense. A well-developed private education service industry—the *juku*—that revolves around preparing students for these examinations has flourished as an adjunct to the formal education system. The majority of Japanese students attend *juku* as well as public school.

The examinations constitute a system of academic selection that is brutal by American standards, and a number of concerns have been raised about the psychological problems of submitting children —most students are twelve years old when they take the high school examination—to such pressures. In one well-documented case, a sixth grader suffered a nervous breakdown while taking the entrance examination for Nada, one of the prestigious secondary schools (White 1987, 142). The ultimate goal of this system is not hard to fathom: "The examination hell sorts the sheep from the goats; a man who can't take the strain would be no use anyway" (Dore 1976).

Clearly, the institutional characteristics that define the Japanese education system hold little comfort for school choice advocates. The educational system that laid the foundation for Japan's economic success is rigidly controlled by a centralized bureaucracy, and any choice of secondary schools is predicated on a highly selective screening system. Again we have a case where choice advocates seem to be willing to use a foreign system to measure how bad America's schools are, but unwilling to use it as an institutional example to emulate. If public education in America is fragmented compared to Germany, it barely rates as a cohesive system when compared to Japan.

Great Britain

In 1988 the government of Margaret Thatcher passed the Education Reform Act (ERA), a sweeping piece of legislation designed to use market economics to improve education. Under the new law, state-funded schools in England and Wales took control of their budgets, an open-enrollment policy was established, and the ability of schools to survive financially was linked to their success in attracting students. "In effect a quasi-market in education was established" (Bowe, Ball, and Gold 1992, 24).

At first glance, Great Britain would appear to be the very model of school choice being argued for in this country. In both places the argument is based in economics. In Britain, support for the ERA drew heavily from the market theories of such economists as Friedrich Hayek and from the delegation argument promoted by writers such as T.J. Peters and R.H. Waterman (1982; also see Bowe, Ball, and Gold 1992, 24). The delegation argument holds that those who actually deliver services are in the best position to allocate appropriate resources effectively and efficiently to meet client demands.

This, of course, is exactly what school choice supporters in the United States are arguing (Chubb and Moe 1988, 1990; Fliegel and MacGuire 1993). Give schools the autonomy to meet their clients' needs—and not those of a bureaucracy—and tie their survival to success in delivering such services, and education will benefit. The market will improve education if only the controlling institutions will allow it to work.

The school choice model in Great Britain, however, stops considerably short of what public choice "purists" such as Chubb and Moe advocate. The ERA gave schools control of their own budgets and tied survival to their ability to attract students, but it did not give schools control over the goals of education. The ERA also established a national curriculum and a national examination system. How schools live up to these standards is, more or less, up to them. They decide where the money is spent and how to implement the curriculum. Accountability for meeting those standards remains in the hands of the national government. This aspect of the British system provides a powerful informational tool. The uniformity of standards provides a yardstick to measure which of the diverse types of schools is succeeding in meeting the nationally mandated standards.

Such a degree of centralization has proven to have some disturbing consequences. Control of the curriculum is at the national level, and education continues to be a focus of legislative attention, not all of it positive. "The intervention by ministers in the prescription of subjects, course content and teaching methods since 1991 has seemed arbitrary, even whimsical" (McLean 1993, 25). Still, a national curriculum and a national examination system are generally considered critical components of school choice in Great Britain. They provide the guide for the educational marketplace. Indeed, British school choice advocates look somewhat askance at their American counterparts for failing to push for similar policies. British and American reformers may use the same terms and the same economic-based arguments; in reality the strategies are quite different. "With regard to policies implementing the language of markets and choice, the Anglo-American contrasts are very sharp" ("Us and Them" 1989).

Such an observation seems quite supportable. A coalition of school choice advocates in the United States demanding uniform national curricula and achievement examinations is hard to imagine. In their prescription for a choice-based system, Chubb and Moe (1990, 225) say that "when it comes to performance, schools are held accountable from below, by parents and students who directly experience their services and are free to choose." Centralizing control over curriculum and achievement examinations even at the state level is in direct opposition to such a vision of school choice.

Even though these constitute important differences, the British system may hold important lessons for any school choice system adopted on this side of the Atlantic. Although held accountable to nationally decided standards, British schools have been vested with a great deal of local autonomy. They seem a fairly good laboratory to examine at least some of the promised benefits of choice. Scholars who have studied the effects of Britain's market-based approach to education have come to mixed conclusions. While success stories certainly exist within the new system, as yet there is no identifiable pattern indicating the market approach is elevating education as a whole.

Because the ERA is a recent innovation—although enacted in 1988, its provisions were not fully implemented until several years later—its ultimate effects are a long way from being decided. There certainly is no firm evidence that school choice has improved or hurt education. Several preliminary conclusions, however, have been made. Bowe,

Ball, and Gold (1992) have produced perhaps the most comprehensive study of the new system. They found that open-enrollment policies coupled with per student funding grievously hurt some schools. The reason is that the supply of students is fixed. In order for one school to attract more students—and more money—another school must lose an equal amount. An immediate and blunt impact of the market system is that "many schools are starting out by losing cash" (Bowe, Ball, and Gold 1990, 29).

Another finding that crosses the Atlantic is the concern with closing schools. To work, the market requires that inefficient and unsuccessful producers be eliminated. While this may work for widget manufacturers, closing schools carries political consequences. "The [Local Education Agency] has never quite been able to bring itself to select one school for closure. Ironically it may well be the fear among local politicians of parental reaction to the closure of their 'local' school, reflected at the ballot box, that produces this unwillingness" (Bowe, Ball, and Gold 1992). In other words, school closures are unlikely to be attributed simply to the efficiencies of the market. Angry parents will seek someone to blame, and such responsibility is usually assigned to a politician. This points out a serious problem in treating education as just another market-provided service. The decision to create an education marketplace is a political one. Politicians will feel the consequence of a school's closure.

Bowe, Ball, and Gold also discovered a number of dangers inherent in transferring industry practices to education. In their interviews with teachers and school administrators, a consistent theme was a concern over the shifting of goals from education to recruitment, money, and survival. Many believed education had importance beyond being another product to be sold and were worried that the values of the market were trivializing a core component of society. "Most teachers are unhappy with the assumption that enrolling parents and educating students is exactly like marketing and producing baked beans" (Bowe, Ball, and Gold 1992, 55).

Most important, Bowe, Ball, and Gold found that decentralization did not solve the problems associated with catering to external constituencies. Instead of the demands of external clients, local autonomy created the problem of conflicting demands among internal constituencies. Teachers divided over resource priorities according to discipline. Teachers and administrators clashed over recruitment versus quality issues. Different coalitions within schools fought to meet conflicting demands made by parents. "The difficulty that emerges . . . is not just deciding who the customer actually is, parents, employers or students or all of these, but which should have priority at any one time" (Bowe, Ball, and Gold 1992, 79). Decentralization did not eliminate the problems around the conflicting goals of clients and controlling institutions, it merely shifted them from a macro to a micro level. The players have changed, but the game remains the same.

Although the approaches are different—especially in the areas of curriculum and achievement examinations—all these findings in the British system hold lessons for the school choice movement in the United States. The effects of inelastic student population, political concerns over school closures, worries among professionals that marketing education and baked beans are fundamentally different prospects, and the micro-level goal conflicts promoted by decentralization are all aspects of school choice that are applicable to both sides of the Atlantic. None of the findings in these areas offers much comfort to school choice advocates.

While the similarities offer little comfort, the dissimilarities offer even less. In adopting a school choice system the British retain a high degree of centralization over educational goals and standards. They retain a centralized bureaucracy to enforce and report these standards, and the controlling democratic institution—Parliament—has viewed such measures as critical to a functioning education market. Although Great Britain may be the country the United States is closest to culturally, it would not be surprising to find American school choice advocates seeking the greatest distance possible between themselves and their British cousins.

Choice in Other Countries

Although this chapter has focused on the education systems in just three countries, there are examples of other approaches within the international community. Great Britain is certainly not the only country to adopt school choice.

In the Netherlands, for example, school choice is enshrined in the constitution and has been a reality for the better part of a century. Under Dutch law (Article 23 of the constitution), anyone can become a provider of education services and receive public funding at an equal level to public-authority schools. This would appear to be a public choice paradise because it sets up an education marketplace with little government interference. Choice should abound, and those who provide the best services should surely have risen to the top. Because choice has been a fact of life for nearly ninety years, by now the efficiencies of the market should have forged the Netherlands into a global education—and economic—powerhouse.

As a consequence of the law, there is indeed a lot of choice in the Netherlands. The average size of an elementary school is only 175 students. There are also gross inefficiencies in administrative overhead, little innovation, and not much variety. "The Dutch experience to date suggests [the] free market model is naive. Even a casual familiarity with Dutch education indicates that, despite the freedom to found and run alternative schools, a relatively uniform curriculum, pedagogy, and structure are the norm" (Louis and van Velzen 1991).

The Dutch education market simply has not functioned as U.S. school choice advocates envision it. Religious affiliation, geographical proximity to the home, and the socioeconomic mix of enrollment are seen as the primary determinants of school selection (Louis and van Velzen 1991; Ambler 1994). This supports the findings reported in the previous chapters. The demand for quality has not played a significant—or even a minor—role in education development in the Netherlands. Taxpayers seem to be more concerned with the cost of supporting a hugely decentralized system with massive duplication.

The Dutch experience with the downsides of school choice is far from unique. A five-nation study—France, the Netherlands, Belgium, Britain and Canada—concluded that a student's classmates are more important to most parents than a school's curriculum (Glenn 1989). While parents want the choice option, they rarely exercise it according to the models of economic theory driving the public choice argument. Choice has been found to accommodate religious diversity, but it appears to affect equity more than quality (Glenn 1989). Regardless of the nation or its construction, the education marketplace appears to fall considerably short of the benefits claimed by its supporters (Ambler 1994). While there does exist some comfort for school choice advocates in the international arena—the British experiment, for example, has shown some positive preliminary indicators—in general such comparisons raise rather than answer questions about the effectiveness of school choice.

Table 8.1

Comparison of Education Systems

Country	National education bureaucracy	National curriculum	Universal access
Germany[a]	No	Yes	No
Japan	Yes	Yes	No
United Kingdom	Yes	Yes	Yes
United States[b]	No	No	Yes

Notes:

[a]Although Germany has no centralized national education bureaucracy, it has very strong state education bureaucracies. There is no official national curriculum in German, but agreements and cooperation among the states has resulted in a de facto one (approximately 70 percent commonality).

[b]There is a federal education agency, the Department of Education. This bureaucracy, however, has little control over state or local education policies.

Conclusion

This chapter has briefly examined the education systems of Germany, Japan, and Great Britain. A summary of school choice in other nations was also presented. Two essential conclusions are drawn from this study. One is that as far as education is concerned, the institutional arrangements among the primary economic competitors of the United States are more centralized and are subject to more control by bureaucracy and democratic institutions than they are in America (see Table 8.1). Second is that where choice has been adopted, it has not functioned as its supporters in the United States have argued it would. Obviously, neither of these conclusions supports the arguments of school choice advocates, and offers no support for Chubb and Moe's institutional theory.

In the absence of truly comparative data, it is difficult in the extreme to say which country provides the "best" education.[6] More important, given the comparatively decentralized system in the United States, it is even harder to say America's system is worse than, say, Japan's. Compared to Japan, the United States has no education "system." It might be more relevant to draw comparisons between Minnesota or Iowa or Alabama and Japan, rather than between the United States as a whole and Japan. Even then, the most centralized and bureaucratic state education system pales in comparison to the Japanese Ministry of Education.

School choice advocates may be able to construct arguments that cultural differences or unique organizational arrangements such as Britain's national curriculum are the reason school choice has not worked in other countries as it would in the United States. While such arguments may have some merit, it would be hard from a comparative standpoint to defend the position that decentralized, market-driven education systems support the dominant global economies. Of the countries examined here, the Dutch have the most laissez-faire education system, and few in America fear the economic encroachment of the Netherlands.[7] On closer examination, the argument that we must decentralize education to gain an equal economic footing with our competitors appears to be specious.

Notes

1. The test measured proficiency in a number of math and science categories such as numbers and operations, geometry, life sciences, and physics. Of the twelve countries involved in the study, the United States never ranked higher than ninth and was often last.

2. Scholars such as Powell argue that institutional constraints, not lack of education, depress voter turnout in the United States.

3. Virtually all of the school choice literature cited in this research makes some mention of the ties between reform and global competition. With a scant handful of notable exceptions (e.g., Best 1993), there is no attention paid to how other countries structure their education systems.

4. There are education systems in Europe that are more decentralized. The Dutch system, for example, is a model of school choice and has been operative for the majority of this century; it is given some attention in this chapter. European countries that represent serious economic competition to the United States tend to have much more centralized systems. France, to present the opposite of the Dutch system, has a rigidly centralized system concentrated at the national level.

5. Two sets of critical examinations are taken during a student's career: one to get into high school and one to get into college.

6. The complications inherent in measuring education performance are compounded by cross-national study. In addition to all the problems with using standardized tests, there are questions of who to test. There are huge variations among education systems. Is an American high school equivalent to a German *Gymnasium* or *Hauptschule*? Are tenth graders equivalent to British fourth formers? American students may suffer in some international comparisons simply because of the more universal nature of this country's education system. Other countries tend to weed out their less able students. The United States seeks to keep them enrolled.

7. While for Americans the Netherlands does not conjure up the same economic fears as Japan or Germany, this country has a successful and diversified economy that provides a high standard of living for its citizens. And whatever the pros or cons of its secondary and elementary education system, the Dutch hold their own in international education comparisons among industrialized nations. For example, the Dutch literacy rate is 99 percent, and ten years of elementary and secondary education is compulsory.

——— Nine ———

Conclusion

Although a powerful and attractive normative argument, the institutional theory has failed virtually every empirical test. No evidence supports the conclusion that massive institutional decentralization and reliance on the marketplace will improve education. The research presented in this book leads to the conclusion that school choice theorists have misidentified the problems with the education system and that their proposed cures are likely to reduce equity without improving performance. Public choice in education simply does not work.

The purpose of this chapter is to bring all the strands of the research together into a cohesive explanation of *why* the institutional theory fails and why school choice will not work. Such an examination may then offer clues toward a more robust and useful explanatory model of education.

Assuming the Worst

The primary reason for the failure of the institutional theory is that it is founded on two a priori assumptions that have dubious empirical support. The first of these is that the American education system is failing. Expressing a common sentiment, Bruce MacLaury, president of the Brookings Institution, says that "by most accounts, the American education system is not working well" (Chubb and Moe 1990, ix). The belief that all education indicators point toward failure is shared not only by school choice advocates but also by much of the public. Yet, as some education scholars are at considerable pains to point out (Bracey 1991, 1992, 1993; Sandia National Laboratories 1993), this view is at best a gross distortion. Most commonly accepted measures show the opposite: American education is *not* failing.

The reality seems to be that the education system is *perceived* as failing. Spurred on by a regular barrage of dismal tidings conveyed by the media, the general pessimism is not surprising. The perception is nonetheless misleading. On virtually every measure available, American education is making gains. Scores on the SAT are not declining, but advancing (Sandia National Laboratories 1993, 267–72). Dropout rates are not increasing—they have, in fact, held steady for the past two decades. Dropout rates may have even been artificially inflated over the past half decade because urban schools have had an influx of immigrants who do not have the background or language skills to succeed (Sandia National Laboratories 1993, 265).

Urban schools are not all caught in an inescapable spiral of decay but are actually making progress in the face of terrific social and financial challenges (Council of the Great City Schools 1992, xiv–xv). Plenty of evidence concludes that American students are holding their own or are even ahead of their international counterparts (Elley 1992). American students are not learning less than previous generations, they are learning more (Bracey 1993). In critical subject areas such as mathematics, American students are not regressing, but making strong advances (National Center for Education Statistics 1992). These gains are even more impressive given the U.S. education system's commitment to universal access.

The deeply entrenched view of American education as failing is a constant source of frustration to a growing segment of education researchers. Finding good news about American education is not difficult. In fact, gathering an impressive stack of scholarly studies that report favorably on the academic achievements of American students during the past decade is a simple task. The problem appears to be that no one pays attention to them. In his annual report on the condition of public education in *Phi Delta Kappan,* Gerald W. Bracey (1993, 105–17) convincingly documents a depressing list of misinterpretations and outright distortions of education performance in America that have been widely circulated by scholars and the media. These to a large extent perform as self-fulfilling prophecies. Everyone knows schools are bad, and anything that contradicts this view must be wrong. Bracey argues that the most dangerous part of continuing to blame schools for failing despite ample evidence to the contrary is that the real problems threatening education—poverty, disintegrating families, and lack of public support—are being ignored.

Without question, the American education system faces serious challenges. The odds are stacked against the education system, espe-cially in urban areas, where the broad and deep problems of society are overwhelming (Kozol 1991). Given the extent of the problems, per-haps what is truly remarkable is not that the American education sys-tem is failing but that it is doing as well as it is.

If one is selective about what studies, or what portions of studies, are used, a convincing list of statistics can be presented pointing to-ward the academic collapse of American education. The assumption that quality education is the primary unmet demand that parents and students place on schools is not even based on questionable, screened statistics. Bluntly, the assumption that a large unmet demand exists among public school parents and students for higher-quality education is manufactured from whole cloth.

Virtually every piece of available evidence indicates that what par-ents and students demand from schools goes far beyond academic excellence. Geographical proximity and the convenience it represents seem to be the primary demand (Elmore 1990). Religious services and the socioeconomic and racial composition of the enrollment seem to be the next most important concern (Glenn 1989; see also chapter five). As for education quality, the vast majority of public opinion polls indicate that this is a demand already met by public schools. The 1993 annual Gallup poll on education indicated that 47 percent of Ameri-cans give their local public schools a grade of A or B. Only 4 percent give public schools a failing grade.[1] Over the past ten years there is no evidence of a loss of faith in quality at public schools. More people gave public schools high grades in 1993 than in 1992 or 1985 or any year in between.

Interestingly, the Gallup poll shows that those who rate public schools the lowest are those with no children in school or with children enrolled in private schools. In other words, those who rate public schools the lowest are the least qualified to make such a judgment. Limiting the responses to public school parents—those who suppos-edly are "demanding" more quality—56 percent give their local schools a grade of A or B. If the question is focused on rating the school a parent's oldest child attends, 72 percent award an A or a B. John Goodlad (1984) reports a survey of 8,624 parents where only 10 percent give their schools a grade of D or lower. "Overall," concludes Goodlad (1984, 36), "the data do not convey the deep parental concern that supposedly has prevailed widely."

The real concern about education springs from the perception that the nation's education system is failing. Asked to assess the nation's public schools as a whole, only 19 percent in the Gallup poll give the grade of A or B. Most people are satisfied with their own public school but are concerned about the failure of everyone else's. Given the oft-reinforced but questionable perception that American education is somehow grinding to a halt, these differences in opinion are perfectly explainable.

Thus little evidence supports the demand assumption from the general public. Most parents seem quite satisfied with their local school. Using evidence taken from public school parents to show they are massively dissatisfied with their public schools is impossible, because there is none.[2] Instead of public schools, the demand assumption rests completely on private schools. School choice advocates and the institutional theory derive much support from the notion that private schools are successful because they offer the quality educational services public schools do not. The empirical evidence argues that this explanation is spurious. Although many private schools no doubt offer top-notch education services, the demands many parents seek to fulfill in the private education sector are for religious services (Brown 1992; see also chapter five), racial segregation (see chapter five), and the "right" socioeconomic status of their children's peers (Glenn 1989; Ambler 1994).

While students at private schools unquestionably score higher on achievement measures (Coleman and Hoffer 1987; Coleman, Hoffer, and Kilgore 1982), this is just as likely to reflect selective screening as the ability to provide superior education services (Witte 1992). Too much contrary evidence exists to accept the argument that private school enrollments are driven primarily by a demand for better education quality than the public system provides.

In sum, the two assumptions that form the basis for the institutional theory and school choice in general are highly suspect. While the assumption of failure may protect itself behind a barricade of dismal media reports and selectively chosen statistics, the assumption of demand is hard pressed to muster a single shred of empirical support to its defense. If, as the evidence suggests, these two assumptions are false, then the institutional theory cannot function. If the existing system is healthy and already meeting the demands of its clientele, it is already providing in large measure the promised benefits of the education market.

Institutionalizing School Choice

The great contribution of Chubb and Moe's institutional theory is that it shifted the focus of education and policy researchers out of the classroom and into the realm of politics (Best 1993). It forced a reexamination of the fundamental institutional arrangements of the American education system. Regardless of its flaws, this was a significant and important contribution.

The chief flaw in the institutional theory is that it failed to ask *if* the education system was failing. Instead, it sought to explain *why* the system was failing. The answer was found in the institutional arrangements of the system. As argued by Chubb and Moe, public education is a monopoly under democratic control. The system seeks to serve the goals of its democratic masters—legislatures and school boards. Between parents, students, and the institutions of democratic control stands an entrenched bureaucracy. This bureaucracy enforces the values of its democratic master and limits the ability of schools to respond to the needs and demands of parents and students. Such a rigid institutional structure, elaborated on in detail (Chubb and Moe 1988, 1990), provides a plausible explanation of why the education system is failing.

Viewed from a different perspective, the existing institutional structure provides an equally plausible explanation of why the system is not failing. Democratic institutions seek to mediate conflicting goals within the broader electorate and advance policies that, at a minimum, are agreeable to a majority and not so obnoxious to the minority that they violate basic rights. The process of balancing costs, demands, and concerns of equity from widely different sectors of society is hardly going to be an efficient one. But if education is a key component of societal—not just individual—success, democratic control makes sense. Democratic control will not produce the efficiencies of the market because democracy is not an efficient process. But democratic institutions should be able to translate conflicting demands into something that broadly advances society's interests. If we are to believe the opinion polls, legislatures and school boards have performed this task admirably.

Control by democratic institutions certainly will not guarantee education's success. Legislatures and school boards have limited control over problems such as disintegrating families, violence, and drugs. What democratic institutions can to some extent guarantee is that the broader education goals of society will be pursued. In the early 1980s a slew of reports sparked a national concern over education. The democratic institutions of education translated those concerns into a varied reform agenda that in many instances improved education performance.

The reforms of the 1980s were not limited to policy. The "monopolistic" and "rigid" public education hierarchy proved quite willing to divest itself of traditional institutional structure. Private companies were hired to run schools in Minnesota and Detroit (Jelier 1993), voucher experiments were begun (Witte 1992), state legislatures everywhere began allowing districts to adopt choice policies (Carnegie Foundation 1992, 99–112), democratic bodies at all levels of education trimmed bloated bureaucracies and reformed in response to citizen demand (e.g., Hess 1991; Payne 1991). None of this quite fits the picture of a monolithic public monopoly committed to the institutional status quo.

In fact, the monopolistic institutional education structure portrayed by some scholars (e.g., Peterson 1990) on closer examination fragments into distinct parts, each with unique institutional characteristics. Represented in the form of organizational structure and policy mandates, these differences have consequences for education performance. Greater democratic control (see chapters four and seven) is not harmful to education performance and may even be beneficial. The reforms promoted by different education systems within the United States vary widely, but often they have positive system-level results (see chapters six and seven).

Ignoring such possibilities, the institutional theory sees only a rigid, top-heavy structure that forces upon students and parents what they do not really want. The market is offered as a solution. Smash the existing structure and use the properties of the market to fulfill demands. If a school's survival depends on attracting students, and attracting students is a function of offering a better education, then a better education for all will result. The argument appears persuasive but erodes quickly when faced with a series of practical difficulties. The market solution assumes parents and students will have enough information to make a decision on what school offers the "best" education. This assumption appears to be patently insupportable (Brown 1992). Not only are the costs involved in obtaining such information considerable, the larger question is whether such information can exist at all in an education marketplace. To provide a comparative yardstick, there must be some uniform measure. In the United Kingdom's public choice system this is provided by a national curriculum and a national achievement test. Both are anathema to the institutional theory (Chubb and Moe 1990, 211). The reason is simple: such uniform regulations cannot exist without a centralized controlling democratic institution to promulgate them and a hierarchical bureaucracy to enforce them. From an educational perspective, the optimal combination, a national achievement test and permitting local districts to experiment with the curriculum, would require an even greater bureaucracy to monitor the experiments and disseminate the results to other schools.

The potential downsides of the market are ignored by the institutional theory. In the abstract, if demand for quality education is the driving force of the market, then quality education will be produced. If, as seems eminently possible, other demands prove profitable—religious, racial, or socioeconomic segregation—those too will be produced. The market also requires that inefficient producers be eliminated. Shuttering schools has political as well as economic consequences. If they are rational, school administrators in the education market should shun students who harm their educational "product." If survival is linked to high performance, no school would logically want students who will lower performance scores. The market might well be a cruel place for the emotionally, physically, and socially handicapped. The solution to prevent selective screening is a rigidly enforced anti-discrimination policy. Again, a democratic institution is required to promulgate such legislation, and a bureaucracy is needed to enforce it.

Even if all these concerns are set aside, the market solution still has drawbacks. Ignoring all empirical evidence to the contrary, if the demand for quality education is the single driving force of the market, agreement on how to achieve such a goal is still not guaranteed. The experience in Great Britain (Bowe, Ball, and Gold 1992) suggests that in locally autonomous schools, conflicts between parents, teachers, students, and school administrators on the goal of quality education are the norm rather than the exception. They differ not just on how to achieve the goal but on what the goal really is. This is exactly the sort of problem democratic institutions are designed to solve.

In sum, the institutional perspective offers a number of fresh insights into the performance of the education system. Approached from the view that the system is failing, an argument can be constructed that plausibly lays the blame on institutional arrangements. Such an explanation does not reflect empirical reality. Approached from the perspective that the system is not failing, another interpretation of the institutional structures finds them much more benign and flexible. This view seems a much closer reflection of the real world. Education provides a key component of society. Democratic control mediates conflicts over the goals of education and allows advancement along a path that is broadly acceptable. Although not efficient, democratic control assures minority views are assimilated and at least makes an attempt to address equity concerns. These controlling institutions seek to translate concerns over education into action and, accordingly, enact policies to reflect societal demand.

Toward Another Theory

Although resting on a weak foundation, the institutional theory was an attractive structure. It packed a universal explanation of education into a nice neat box. Sifting through the rubble left by the empirical wrecking ball, it is easy to identify the poor construction materials that contributed to the theory's collapse. A much more difficult task is the reconstruction project. As Chubb and Moe (1990, 565) rhetorically ask their critics, "Is there an alternative theory . . . that can pull together the many factors and offer a coherent explanation of schools?"

Currently the answer is no. But this is not a reason to substitute no theory for a false and misleading one. The reality of education seems to be much messier than that portrayed by the institutional theory. The series of counterhypotheses presented in this literature do not neatly fit together in a seamless theoretical structure. While not as attractive as the institutional theory, they seem a good deal more functional.

Four main theoretical building blocks can be drawn from our research. One is that education in the United States does not consist of a single cohesive, hierarchical system. Instead, it consists of many hierarchical systems. The degree of democratic control, bureaucratic centralization, and local autonomy varies from state to state, from district to district, even from school to school. So much variation exists that portraying the system as uniform and giving components (e.g., school boards and legislatures) the same predictable roles does violence to reality. Any theory seeking a universal explanation of education must account for its variation, not its uniformity.

A second building block is a clearer idea of the role of bureaucracy.

School choice advocates often view bureaucracy in normative terms—bureaucracy is simply bad. In reality, the concept of bureaucracy seems neither inherently good nor evil. Building bureaucratic empires for their own sake is no way to improve education. Enforcing standards and addressing the external pressures of societal problems is. Bureaucracy is a much more complex concept than its portrayal as a producer of red tape suggests. Although it goes against the prevailing normative bias, bureaucracy often has a legitimate and useful function (Goodsell 1994). All education systems—from individual schools to nations—have well-developed bureaucracies. Any useful theory of education must rely much more on bureaucratic theory and much less on ideology. Bureaucracy is a complex, multidimensional concept. As our research has indicated, treating bureaucracy as anything else may fit normative biases but is unlikely to explain empirical reality.

The third building block is the importance of a macro-level perspective on education. The institutional theory approaches education from a micro-level perspective. This bottom-up approach begins with the individual and asks why is the system failing to meet individual needs? The macro, top-down approach begins with the system and asks whether it is meeting its societal obligations. The view from the top brings into sharper focus the role of education beyond the demands of the individual. While individual needs are and should be an important concern, education has a broader societal role. This recognition comes more easily from the macro approach.

The fourth building block is that no single demand drives education. A theory assuming that superior academic standards is the uniform goal of parents is playing to vanity rather than reality. The demands placed on education are more complex and muddier. Some of these demands (e.g., racial segregation and religious indoctrination) are deemed by society to be too offensive to majorities or minorities to be met by public schools. Democratic institutions will seek to ensure such demands are not met. Markets will almost certainly seek to ensure they are.

Policy Recommendations

Herbert Simon (1957) contends that the social sciences are concerned, not with how things are, but how they might be. Our research suggests a number of options that would be profitable for education. The first of these directly contradicts much of the school choice literature—a call for more, not less, uniformity. Currently we have at best rough yardsticks for education quality and performance. No single, comparative indicator can judge schools or students. In the absence of such a measure, the best hope of social science is to limit ignorance rather than increase knowledge. Considerable political forces—not just school choice advocates—resist a mandated national achievement test or a national curriculum. Until we have one or both we are missing a true yardstick of education. We can use SATs or similar measures as estimates of one element in education performance, but until uniform, comparative data are available, the accuracy of our estimates is unknown. Making policy is difficult if you are unsure of what or where the problem is, and judging policy is even harder if you are unsure how or if the problem was affected. A uniform achievement test and a more unified curriculum will help provide a clearer picture of the true condition of education.

A second recommendation is for more centralization within education systems. Within the United States and abroad there is overwhelming evidence that more centralized systems perform better. Centralization seems to increase the ability to set and enforce high academic standards. In essence, centralized systems are better equipped to manipulate the internal-controllable determinants of education. The systems that maximize this form of control tend to have higher performance. In short, systems with higher expectations of education performance by and large fulfill them. This is not necessarily a call for a more entrenched bureaucratic hierarchy. The British experiment has shown that local autonomy and centralized goals are not mutually exclusive concepts. American education is unlikely to be centralized at the national level in any substantive area in the near future. Increased centralization at the state level is already occurring and appears to have had a beneficial effect on education performance.

A third recommendation is for all states to adopt the top-down policies that have demonstrably positive effects. Teacher certification, graduation tests, and smaller learning environments are consistently linked with higher performance. States that have not adopted such measures should be encouraged to do so.

A fourth recommendation is to keep education under the control of democratic institutions. These have been shown to be quite flexible organizational arrangements. During the past decade school boards and legislatures have generated a huge amount of innovation. Everything from longer semesters to school-based management has found a place in the reform kaleidoscope. The experience of systems overseas shows that school choice leads to less, not more, innovation. Nothing in the huge variety of reform approaches being pursued at all levels in this country dispels such beliefs. While seeking meaningful change, democratic institutions also are willing to address equity, even if they are unable to guarantee it. The market seeks efficiency. Equity is not efficient.

The Far from Final Word

The school choice debate is unlikely to be silenced, or even moderately hushed, by any single piece of research. It is driven by ideology, not facts. Our study will have succeeded if it adds a loud empirical voice to the ongoing argument. The data show that the public would be better served to move away from the undeniable lure of school choice ideology. Its tantalizing simplicity fails to address the complex reality of education in America today. Worse, it is antidemocratic. Education, like the concepts of liberty and freedom, is too valuable a commodity to be marketed to the highest bidder.

Notes

1. The "25th Annual Phi Delta Kappa/Gallup Poll of Public Attitudes toward Schools" is reported in Bracey (1993).

2. One convincing piece of evidence that the public is satisfied with its schools comes from the series of referendums on school choice that have been held in various states during the past few years. Choice has been uniformly rejected.

───── Ten ─────

Epilogue: Last Choice

There is always a well-known solution to every problem—
neat, plausible and wrong.

—H.L. Mencken

As a last-stand defense, advocates of choice are fond of pointing toward its grassroots popularity. The people should be given choice because they want choice. Many opinion polls do indicate that the notion of choice is widely supported, so in a democratic society such an argument should be granted some credence. Certainly in our interviews from across the Milwaukee education mosaic, choice was at least initially given a favorable response.

Although getting a generally positive reception, paradoxically school choice was not a topic that quickly arose in our interviews. In fact, despite the ongoing school choice pilot projects in Milwaukee, none of those interviewed voluntarily introduced the subject of school choice. Asked what could be done to improve education, most people brought up in one form or another the same list of changes pursued as part of the reform effort of the 1980s: teacher certification, tougher academic standards, more funding, and smaller class size. These are the same policies, of course, that supporters of choice usually dismiss as ineffective window dressing.

There were two other common components to most people's reform agenda: greater parental involvement and safer environments for students. Safer schools and more concerned parents seem to be held as crucial to improved education quality and performance. They are also generally beyond the control of education policymakers. No school can issue their students a set of parents committed to education. No school can eliminate gangs, drugs, poverty, dysfunctional families, societal prejudices, or many of the other contributors to violence among school-age adolescents. While many schools are seeking to address these two concerns through education and outreach programs, they cannot be expected to take the responsibility of curing societal problems that stretch well beyond the boundaries of the schoolyard. Blaming them for failing to solve these problems is to vilify the messenger while ignoring the message.

Nobody included choice in his or her initial reform proposals. Without exception, choice was a subject introduced by the interviewer. For all its supposed grassroots support, school choice was far down the list of most of our subjects' ideas of education reform. Indeed, it failed to make these lists at all without prompting. People who were directly involved in the Milwaukee choice experiment, or who belonged to schools that wanted to be involved in choice programs, opted first to talk about what they saw as superior characteristics associated with the schools involved in the program rather than the notion of choice itself. What did they consider superior about the choice schools? Smaller class size, higher academic standards, more parental involvement, and safer environments. No one was able to articulate clearly how a market-based system of education could provide these universal wants to everyone without creating segregation or schools for the "leftovers." Institutional arrangements were given only minor attention.

Improving education is a messy business, far messier than the theory and number crunching of social science would seem to suggest. To reinforce this point, we want to end this book as we began it—by letting those who are on the receiving end of the education debate tell their views of what is wrong with education and what can be done to improve it. In each case, the idea of choice is attractive to the individual. The reality of choice seems more problematical.

Kourtney, Student, Riverside High School (MPS)

Kourtney is a sophomore who lives and attends school in Milwaukee's inner city. He is polite, quick with his answers, and seems to have a quality that is missing from many of his peers—hope.

Kourtney is generally positive in his comments about the education he is getting, although he has some suggestions for improvement, such as better teachers and a more motivational classroom environment. "Sometimes I sit in the classroom and the book is so boring. I won't read the book, I'll fall asleep, it's so boring."

Kourtney says it would also be good if all students were guaranteed a textbook, a pen, and a notebook. "We need proper equipment the most—sometimes we have eight- or nine-year-old textbooks."

Asked whether he would like the ability to choose his school, Kourtney responds positively. He says he would like to try going to Rufus King, the magnet school. Did he or his family make any effort to get selected in the lottery for enrollment at King? He gives an unclear response to the question. He says he would like to try some of the college prep courses at King. He also mentions that he has a lot of friends at King and would like the opportunity to spend more time with them.

Would he consider choosing a suburban school? Kourtney says probably not. He says the racial composition of the student body would be an important part of his decision, and most suburban schools are white.

Dalia, Eighth Grade (MPS)

Dalia is somewhat shy, especially in the presence of several older boys who are being interviewed at the same time. To begin with, she has to be asked questions directly, but as she warms to the subject she becomes more animated and joins in a freewheeling give-and-take.

Dalia has a long list of things she wants improved with her school. Like Kourtney, she believes more money to buy better equipment is a basic starting point. She talks about up-to-date textbooks, money for educational field trips, and computers—lots and lots of computers. "A big problem with schools is that they don't have enough funds. We've had one or two field trips for a whole school year," she says.

Her list grows to include better teachers, smaller class size, more classes to choose from. Asked if she would like to be able to choose the school she would attend, she says yes immediately. What school would she go to? One that has all the things on her list. What school is that? She is not quite sure. How would she find out what school has all the things on her list? Again, she is not sure.

Antoninette, Student, Hamilton High School

During an interview with four students that lasts more than an hour, Antoninette stays mostly silent. When she does offer suggestions for improving her academic experience, and education quality in general, they mostly relate to race. The single exception is when she is asked whether schools or parents are the most important contributor to academic success. "Parents are definitely more important," she says.[1]

Pressed for a suggestion on what would improve her education, she says, "More black teachers." Would more minority teachers add cultural diversity, make her feel more comfortable in the classroom, be more approachable, offer a motivational role model? No. "They'd give me better grades." White students get better grades from white teachers, she says, so black teachers should give black students better grades. When the topic of choice is brought up, it does not seem to interest her at all.

David, Student, Riverside High School

David is an easygoing ninth grader who has an honest student's opinion about school: school is a place more to be endured than enjoyed. He does, however, have a clear idea of how to make school a better place. Simply put, make school a closer place. "Change the position of school. I'd like it closer to home, especially during the winter when it gets very cold."

Another way to make school a more tolerable burden, says David, is to cut down on the homework. If he could be put in charge of all education reform, he would halve the weekly extra-classroom assignments. "I can't do all this homework," he says. Sometimes it consists of three or more hours of academic labor a night. There are more important things to be done during your free time. Other improvements under David's education reform regime would include more school dances. After all that work, a little more play deserves official sanction.

Turning more serious, David can quickly recite more or less the same list that Kourtney and Dalia gave. He adds a few original suggestions. Not only does he call for better teachers but more teachers—two per class. That way, even small classes can be taught to students with differing abilities. A teacher will not be forced into pacing a class to the hypothetical average student while boring some students and confusing others. David also wants the curriculum changed so you can always get the classes you want. Some classes tend to fill up quickly, and you end up taking courses that really do not interest you.

Introduced to the idea of school choice, David translates it to curriculum choice. He would like to go to a school where the good classes are still open and available for him. "A place where you can pick the classes you take," he says. He would prefer, however, to stay where he is. His friends are all at Riverside.

Chanto, Eleventh Grade, Hamilton High School

Chanto, a Chapter 220 student, is engaging and upbeat about the education he is receiving. Good teachers, lots of challenging homework, and a safe environment—Chanto says he has this at Hamilton and is grateful for it. He agrees with some of his fellow 220 students that there is some racial tension between them and their suburban classmates, but unlike many of the others, he does not continually refer to race when discussing education.

Chanto seems indifferent to choice. It might work, he says, but it would depend on a lot of things going right and would require a lot of government monitoring. He is intrigued, however, by the idea of introducing competition and incentives as spurs for increased education performance. He thinks choice is targeting the wrong people; instead of schools facing the incentives and punishments of the market, it should be students.

Students have a fundamental grasp of capitalism, Chanto says, and there exists a much simpler way to improve their academic performance than school choice—simply pay them for attendance and grades. "Pay kids to go to school. A dollar a day if you keep a certain grade," he says. Chanto's plan is designed to help students take their studies more seriously by creating concrete rewards for superior performance. He says that is a market system students would understand and respond to.

Kathleen Bogdan, Director of Development, St. Joan Antida High School

Kathy Bogdan is an energetic administrator who carries an aura of efficiency. Without reference she can quickly roll off statistics on St. Joan's enrollment (340), the average size of a graduating class (90), the portion of that class that goes on to college (89 percent), and the amount of scholarships, grants, and similar financial aid they will be awarded (approximately $300,000). She is quick to give visitors a detailed tour including stops at a small but well-equipped library, a computer lab, and classes in session. There are also discussions of internship programs, specialized-skills classes, and individual career counseling. St. Joan's is serious about education, and Kathy Bogdan is serious about St. Joan's.

She sees school choice as an opportunity for students to get to schools like St. Joan's. She says, "This is the best example of what choice could do; it could offer a lot of opportunities." Bogdan does not attempt to portray the public school system as an abject failure—she has close family teaching in Milwaukee schools and is well acquainted with the problems they face—but she believes St. Joan's has something unique to offer.

This includes single-sex education. The all-girls environment is promoted in a recruiting flyer as a place where "a girl acquires higher educational goals and a greater self-concept." It also includes a dress code and more discipline than is found in most public schools. "And we'd never apologize for that," Bogdan says. "We can set rules and make people abide by them, that's an important lesson in itself." It also includes mandatory religious education. Of the twenty-four required credits of the St. Joan's curriculum, three are in theology.

While strongly believing school choice should be expanded to allow public school students an opportunity to attend schools like St. Joan's, Bogdan does not see choice as a panacea. She is fully cognizant that although St. Joan's has a highly liberal enrollment policy—virtually no one is turned away—it is not prepared for some of the difficulties faced by public schools in educating problem students and those with specialized needs. The real beneficiaries of school choice, whether it becomes a reality or not, will be not only St. Joan's and its new pool of students but also the public schools. "Maybe be the best thing about choice is that it will force [public schools] to take a long, hard look at themselves," she said.

Rick, Guidance Counselor, Washington High

Rick has been working as a guidance counselor in the Milwaukee Public Schools for twenty years. Washington High is the computer magnet school in Milwaukee. Rick repeated many of the reforms the students noted but focused on discipline and teachers. When asked about school choice, he responded with information about the impact of the Chapter 220 program on the suburbs: "220 kids who go to the suburbs arrive with an attitude. They know the school is getting several thousand dollars in aid because of them. Some of these districts, like [a declining suburb], need the money pretty badly. 220 students know that won't be disciplined because they might transfer. They get away with things we won't tolerate in MPS." To Rick, choice would exacerbate the discipline problems that he faced on a daily basis. Unless parents were actively involved, a student could blackmail the school. Teachers and principals would become timid if funding for the school meant they had to keep troublemakers happy.

Sarah, Graduate, St. Francis High

We were struck by the problem that Rick raised. By making students and parents the equivalent of consumers in a marketplace, might the marketplace leverage be used to prevent some schools from performing as well as they can? In short, is there a market for low-quality education? To confirm the problem of discipline linked to the 220 choice program, we interviewed Sarah, age nineteen, a recent high school graduate of St. Francis High. St. Francis is a working-class suburb south of Milwaukee. Sarah reinforced Rick's claims by saying that "220 students got it made. Teachers know they can't punish them." The transfer students, in her words, "get away with murder." What sort of things? "Being late, wearing [gang] colors, talking back to teachers." Asked if she thought there was a double standard in applying discipline, Sarah replied, "Yes."

A Final Anecdote

In July 1994 U.S. high school students provided a stunning rebuttal to the notion that America's educational system was failing. At the 35th International Mathematical Olympiad in Hong Kong, the United States shocked the teams from other nations, not just by winning but winning by an unprecedented margin. They did so because each of the six team members scored a perfect score on the two-day examination, a feat never before accomplished at the Olympiad. Despite training as a group for only one month (compared to the year-round tutoring and practicing of some national teams), the U.S. team routed those of sixty-nine other countries. All six U.S. team members went to public schools ("Education: A U.S. Gold Medal in Math" 1994).

Conclusion

Given the array of problems they face, public schools would probably do well to "take a long, hard look at themselves." And, in many cases, they are doing exactly that. The Milwaukee Public School system, for example, is engaged in a rigorous self-analysis, publicizing its failures and experimenting with reforms.[2] It is also at the forefront of the school choice movement. The MPS relies on voluntary magnet schools, participates in voluntary cross-district busing with suburban schools (the 220 program), and competes against private schools in the state's experimental choice program.

Perhaps, as Kathy Bogdan argues, some form of school choice may have a role to play in such reform efforts. The anecdotal evidence gathered by our interviews, however, indicates that there is no real depth of support for the school choice option. People seem to be attracted to school choice owing to its positive connotations of individual freedom. Arguing that people favor school choice because they favor individual freedom is like saying that people oppose school choice because they favor government by democracy. Few are going to register negative opinions about democracy as an abstract idea, even though they may have lengthy litanies about the failures of their democratically controlled governments. If school choice were presented as an end to democratic control of education—which is exactly what Chubb and Moe argue—it would likely put a much less positive spin on first responses to the choice label. As Jeffrey Henig (1994, 184) says, "Chubb and Moe's identification of majoritarianism as the source of the problem is somewhat unusual. More common is the view that majorities are the source of legitimacy in democratic policies. . . ."

The point is that high ratings for "choice" are an easily breached final redoubt for school choice. Once beyond the label, individual opinions on school choice become less positive and much more complex. Our interviews indicate that, on the individual level, choice confuses as much as it illuminates. It offers one sign for a multitude of paths, some of which travel in opposite directions. School choice ultimately fails because its simple answers do not address the complex questions raised by the people it is designed to save.

Notes

1. Hamilton School District officials agree. At the time of our interviews they were engaged in a highly sophisticated series of surveys attempting to gauge what parents and the public in general knew about their schools. They intend to use this information to establish better lines of communication with parents.

2. These efforts include teaching initiatives, parental outreach plans, and innovative programs such as School to Work and Equity 2000. These and other goals are outlined in the annual *Report Card to the Community* issued by the MPS.

Appendix

Statistical Tables

Table A.1

Communications Test

(Dependent variable = percentage of cohort passing
standardized communications test)

Variable	Fifth grade	Eighth grade	Tenth grade
Organization			
Size of bureaucracy	−1.097*	−2.056*	−1.241
Elected superintendent	.986	−.793	1.227
Percentage disciplined	−.093	−.137	.071
Percentage staff resigning	−.269	−.516	−.027
Competition			
Percentage students in private schools	−.887*	−1.114*	.065
Percentage in gifted classes	.853	2.061*	.878
Controls			
Cohort's previous pass rate	.207*	.295*	.462*
Family income	.007*	.009*	.003*
Madison School District	—	—	−16.078*
Constant	48.101*	28.990*	21.836*
R^2	.46	.67	.68
Adjusted R^2	.39	.62	.63
F	6.06	14.23	13.09
N	64	64	64

*$p < .05$. Unstandardized coefficients reported.

Table A.2

Math Test

(Dependent variable = percentage of cohort passing standardized math test)

Variable	Fifth grade	Eighth grade	Tenth grade
Organization			
Size of bureaucracy	−1.151	−.513	1.399
Elected superintendent	−.754	−1.290	1.588
Percentage disciplined	−.049	−.137	.027
Percentage staff resigning	−.258	−.436	.272
Competition			
Percentage students in private schools	−.525*	−1.188*	.119
Percentage in gifted classes	2.174*	2.246*	.139
Controls			
Cohort's previous pass rate	.339*	.197	.419*
Family income	.006*	.008*	−.001
Madison School District	−23.033*	—	—
Jefferson School District	—	—	−26.604*
Constant	48.101*	28.990*	21.836*
R^2	.46	.67	.68
Adjusted R^2	.39	.62	.63
F	6.06	14.23	13.09
N	64	64	64

*$p < .05$. Unstandardized coefficients reported.

Table A.3

Determinants of Bureaucracy

(Dependent variable = number of bureaucrats per student)

Independent variables	Slope	Beta	t-Score
Number of schools per capita	4.628	.53	5.97*
Percentage students on free lunch program	.014	.12	1.59
Elected superintendent	−.492	−.19	2.48*
Average teacher salary	−.234	−.35	4.69*
Expenditures per student	.005	.14	1.96
Glades School District	2.657	.26	4.04*
Union School District	1.971	.20	3.19*
Constant	4.31		
R^2	.78		
Adjusted R^2	.73		
F	30.26		
N	66		

*$p < .05$.

Table A.4

Determinants of Private School Enrollment

(Dependent variable = percentage of students in private schools)

Variable	Coefficient	Standard error	t-Score
Math model			
Lagged private school enrollment	.940	.010	93.63*
Lagged public school performance	.004	.004	1.03
Black enrollment percentage	.007	.002	2.58*
Percentage Catholic population	.016	.006	2.44*
Family income	−.000	−.000	−.170
Constant	−.390	.405	−.960
Estimated ρ	−.024		
R^2	.98		
Adjusted R^2	.98		
N	329		

*$p < .05$.

Table A.5

Determinants of Private School Enrollment

(Dependent variable = percentage of students in private schools)

Variable	Coefficient	Standard error	t-Score
Communications model			
Lagged private school enrollment	.930	.010	88.3*
Lagged public school performance	−.000	.006	−.08
Black enrollment percentage	.007	.002	2.66*
Percentage Catholic population	.014	.006	2.26*
Family income	.000	.000	.56
1987 dummy	.054	.086	.63
1988 dummy	−.149	.087	−1.71
1989 dummy	−.112	.095	−1.19
1990 dummy	−.128	.096	−1.33
Constant	−.021	.593	−.04
Estimated ρ	−.019		
R^2	.98		
Adjusted R^2	.98		
N	329		

*$p < .05$.

Table A.6

Variable Effects over Time

(Reported coefficient: effect of independent variable on dependent variable)

Lag (years)	Lagged private school enrollment	Lagged public school performance	Black enrollment percentage	Percentage Catholic population	Family income
Communications model					
2	.87*	.001	.007*	.024*	.000
3	.80*	.024	.019*	.040*	.000
4	.75*	.031*	.025*	.063*	.000
Math model					
2	.88*	.072	.012*	.026*	.000
3	.82*	.012*	.016*	.046*	.000
4	.76*	.025*	.022*	.068*	.000

Note: Unstandardized coefficient taken from fully specified models.
*$p < .05$.

Table A.7

Determinants of Public School Performance

(Dependent variable = percentage of students passing standardized test)

Variable	Coefficient	Standard error	t-Score
Math model			
Cohort's previous pass rate	.299	.052	5.69*
Lagged private school enrollment	−.370	.211	−1.76
Lagged public school performance	.170	.074	2.42*
Percent in gifted classes	.615	.479	1.28
Family income	.000	.000	.358
Percent receiving free lunches	-.025	.085	-.289
Bradford School District dummy	−1.49	5.41	-.276
Madison School District dummy	−14.44	5.30	−2.72*
1989 dummy	1.72	.88	1.95
1990 dummy	−.45	1.01	−.446
Constant	50.67	8.41	6.02*
R^2	.32		
Adjusted R^2	.29		
N	198		

*$p < .05$. GLS coefficients reported.

Table A.8

Determinants of Public School Performance

(Dependent variable = percentage of students passing standardized test)

Variable	Coefficient	Standard error	t-Score
Communications model			
Cohort's previous pass rate	.114	.036	3.13*
Lagged private school enrollment	−.227	.095	−2.39*
Lagged public school performance	.463	.063	7.35*
Percentage in gifted classes	.195	.244	.80
Family income	.000	.000	1.08
Percentage receiving free lunches	−.046	.041	−1.12
Constant	41.25	6.10	6.75*
Estimated ρ	−.194		
R^2	.45		
Adjusted R^2	.43		
N	198		

*$p < .05$.

Table A.9

Variable Effects over Time

(Reported coefficient: effect of independent variable on dependent variable)

Lag (years)	Previous pass rate	Lagged private school enrollment	Lagged public school performance	Percentage in gifted classes	Family income	Free lunch recipients
Communications model						
2	.10*	−.315*	.329*	.390	.000	−.072
3	.13*	−.299*	.334*	.327	.000	.071
4	.139*	−.289*	.218*	.416*	.000	−.067
Math model						
2	.24*	−.429	.146	.693	.000	−.039
3	.295*	−.248	.193*	.595	.000	−.039
4	.306	−.264	.207*	.551	.000	−.039

Note: Unstandardized coefficient taken from fully specified models. Math model coefficients are generated by GLS procedure.
*$p < .05$.

Table A.10

Determinants of Public School Performance by Ethnic Group

(Dependent variable = percentage of students passing standardized test)

Variable	White	Black
Math model		
Cohort's previous pass rate	.164*	.519*
Lagged private school enrollment	.052	.296
Lagged public school performance	.436*	.336*
Percentage in gifted classes	.391	.543
Family income	−.000	−.000
Percentage receiving free lunches	.050	.005
1989 dummy	—	6.74*
1990 dummy	—	2.23*
Constant	35.79	27.22*
Estimated ρ	−.40*	−.17
R^2	.36	.38
Adjusted R^2	.34	.34
N	198	127

*$p < .05$. Unstandardized coefficients reported.

Table A.11

Determinants of Public School Performance by Ethnic Group

(Dependent variable = percentage of students passing standardized test)

Variable	White	Black
Communications model		
Cohort's previous pass rate	.051*	.197*
Lagged private school enrollment	.004	.173
Lagged public school performance	.380*	.515*
Percentage in gifted classes	.350	.137
Family income	.000	−.000
Percentage receiving free lunches	.019	−.105
1989 dummy	—	8.32*
1990 dummy	—	5.67*
Constant	50.06*	33.38*
Estimated ρ	−.13	−.12
R^2	.26	.39
Adjusted R^2	.24	.35
N	198	127

*$p < .05$. Unstandardized coefficients reported.

Table A.12

Variable Effects over Time: Math Model by Ethnic Group

(Reported coefficient: effect of independent variable on dependent variable)

Lag (years)	Previous pass rate	Lagged private school enrollment	Lagged public school performance	Percentage in gifted classes	Family income	Free lunch recipients
Black						
2	.472*	.255	.367*	.372	.000	.026
3	.510*	.249	.252*	.862	.000	.026
4	.632*	.376	.177*	.971	.001*	−.004
White						
2	.138*	.053	.374*	.584	−.000	−.065
3	.170*	.084	.448*	.536	−.000	.068
4	.182*	.059	.442*	.602*	.000	.065

Note: Unstandardized coefficient taken from fully specified models.
*$p < .05$.

Table A.13

Variable Effects over Time: Communications Model by Ethnic Group

(Reported coefficient: effect of independent variable on dependent variable)

Lag (years)	Previous pass rate	Lagged private school enrollment	Lagged public school performance	Percentage in gifted classes	Family income	Free lunch recipients
Black						
2	.281*	.126	.195*	.480	−.000	−.150
3	.265*	.010	.201*	.567	−.000	−.168
4	.287*	.076	.130*	.586	−.001*	−.157
White						
2	.051	.020	.155*	.565*	.000	.037
3	.051*	.020	.155*	.536*	.000	.030
4	.097*	.077	−.087	.611*	.000	.037

Note: Unstandardized coefficient taken from fully specified models.

*p < .05.

Table A.14

Determinants of State-Level Education Performance

(Dependent variable = 1988 Standardized Education Index model)

Variable	1980 Lag		1984 Lag		1986 Lag	
	Coefficient	t-Score	Coefficient	t-Score	Coefficient	t-Score
Lagged SEI	.836	19.39**	.847	25.62**	.903	39.18**
Graduation test	.824	2.97*	.499	2.37*	.104	.76
Students per school	−.003	−2.97*	−.003	−3.90*	−.002	−3.15*
Logged teacher/student ratio	1.29	1.24	1.76	2.59*	1.03	2.28*
NTE test	.188	.78	.200	1.07	.257	2.07*
Number units required for diploma	.016	1.13	.084	1.71	.011	1.49
State-to-district bureaucracy ratio	.104	1.61	.084	1.71	.030	.83
Compulsory school starting age	.047	.32	.052	.45	.002	.03
Constant	6.43	1.91	4.54	1.73	2.70	1.53
N	48		48		48	
R^2	.94		.96		.98	

$*p = .05$; $**p < .01$. Unstandardized coefficients reported.

Table A.15

Determinants of State-Level Education Performance, 1981–90

(Dependent variable = Standardized Education Index [SEI])

Variable	Coefficient	Standard error	t-Score
Public choice	−.866	.209	−4.52*
Graduation test	.598	.132	4.52*
Teacher certification	.234	.102	2.27*
Teacher/pupil ratio	−.068	.029	−2.32*
Students per school	−.0001	.000	−.20
Per pupil expenditures	−.033	.011	−2.99*
Private school enrollment	.020	.015	1.80
Elected education official	.399	.192	2.07*
Teacher/staff ratio	.020	.014	1.48
Teen birthrate	−.004	.005	−.80
Trend	.099	.013	7.18*
1980 SEI	.890	.022	39.27*
Constant	−.856	.683	−1.25
R^2	.950	—	—
Adjusted R^2	.949	—	—
ρ	.58	—	—
N	500		

*$p < .05$. GLS coefficients reported.

References

Adler, Michael; Petch, Alison; and Tweedie, Jack. 1989. *Parental Choice and Education Policy.* Edinburgh: Edinburgh University Press.

Allen, Jeanne. 1991. "Nine Phoney Assertions about School Choice: Answering the Critics." *Heritage Foundation Backgrounder.* September 13.

Ambler, John S. 1994. "Who Benefits from Educational Choice? Some Evidence from Europe." *Journal of Policy Analysis and Management* 13:454–76.

Astin, A. 1971. *Predicting Academic Performance.* New York: Free Press.

Bainbridge, William, and Sundre, Steven. 1991. "School Choice: The Education Issue of the 1990s." *Children Today*, January/February.

Best, John Hardin. 1993. "Perspectives on Deregulation of Schooling in America." *British Journal of Educational Studies* 41:122–33.

Blalock, Herbert M. 1964. *Causal Inferences in Nonexperimental Research.* Chapel Hill: University of North Carolina Press.

Boswell, John G. 1990. "Improving Our Schools: Parental Choice Is Not Enough." *The World & I*, February.

Bowe, Richard; Ball, Stephen J.; and Gold, Anne. 1992. *Reforming Education and Changing Schools.* New York: Routledge.

Bracey, Gerald W. 1991. "Why Can't They Be Like We Were?" *Phi Delta Kappan* 73:104–17.

———. 1992. "Second Bracey Report on the Condition of Education." *Phi Delta Kappan* 74:104–17.

———. 1993. "Third Bracey Report on the Condition of Education." *Phi Delta Kappan* 75:138–47.

Bridge, R. Gary; Judd, Charles; and Moock, Peter. 1979. *The Determinants of Educational Outcomes.* Cambridge, MA: Ballinger.

Brown, Byron W. 1992. "Why Governments Run Schools." *Economics of Education Review* 11: 287–300.

Bryk, Anthony S., and Lee, Valerie E. 1992. "Is Politics the Problem and Markets the Answer? An Essay Review of Politics, Markets and America's Schools." *Economics of Education Review* 11: 439–51.

Bryk, Anthony S.; Lee, Valerie E.; and Smith, Julia L. 1990. "High School Organization and Its Effects on Teachers and Students: An Interpretive Summary of the Research." In *Choice and Control in American Education*, ed. William H. Clune and John F. Witte. New York: Falmer Press.

Carnegie Foundation for the Advancement of Teaching. 1992. *School Choice.* Princeton, NJ: Carnegie Foundation.

Carr, Robert W. 1991. "Markets Can't Fix Schools' Problems." *Wall Street Journal*, May 2.

Celis, William. 1993. "Uneven Progress in Decade of School Reform." *New York Times,* April 28.

Chira, Susan. 1993. "Lessons of South Carolina: What Secretary May Try for U.S. Schools." *New York Times,* March 24.

Chriss, Barbara; Nash, Greta; and Stern, David. 1992. "The Rise and Fall of Choice in Richmond, California." *Economics of Education Review* 11:395–406.

Chubb, John E., and Moe, Terry. 1988. "Politics, Markets and the Organization of American Schools." *American Political Science Review* 82:1065–89.

———. 1990. *Politics, Markets and America's Schools.* Washington, DC: Brookings Institution.

Coleman, James, et al. 1966. *Equality of Educational Quality.* Washington, DC: Government Printing Office.

Coleman, James, and Hoffer, Thomas. 1987. *Public and Private High Schools.* New York: Basic Books.

Coleman, James; Hoffer, Thomas; and Kilgore, Sally. 1982. *High School Achievement.* New York: Basic Books.

Corcoran, T.B. 1985. "Effective Secondary Schools." In *Reaching for Excellence: An Effective Schools Sourcebook,* ed. R.M.J. Kyle. Washington, DC: Government Printing Office.

Council of the Great City Schools. 1992. *National Urban Education Goals: Baseline Indicators, 1990–1991.* Washington, DC: Council of the Great City Schools.

Daft, Richard L., and Becker, Selwyn W. 1980. "Managerial, Institutional and Technical Influences on Administration: A Longitudinal Analysis." *Social Forces* 59:392–413.

De Witt, Karen. 1993. "College Board Scores Are Up for Second Consecutive Year." *New York Times,* August 19.

Dore, Roald. 1976. *The Diploma Disease.* Berkeley: University of California Press.

Downs, Anthony. 1966. *Inside Bureaucracy.* Boston: Little, Brown.

"Eastern Pendulum Swings Back to Western Selection." 1990. *Times Educational Supplement,* no. 3879:14.

"Education: A U.S. Gold Medal in Math." 1994. *Newsweek,* August 1, p. 63.

Elley, Warwick B. 1992. *How in the World Do Students Read?* Hamburg: International Association for the Evaluation of Educational Achievement.

Elmore, Richard F. 1990. "Choice as an Instrument of Public Policy: Evidence from Education and Health Care." In *Choice and Control in American Education,* vol. 1, ed. William H. Clune and John F. Witte. New York: Falmer Press.

Ferguson, Ronald F. 1991. "Paying for Public Education: New Evidence on How and Why Money Matters." *Harvard Journal on Legislation.* Summer.

Fliegel, Seymour, and MacGuire, James. 1993. *Miracle in East Harlem.* New York: Random House.

Friedkin, Noah E., and Necochea, Juan. 1988. "School Size and Performance: A Contingency Perspective." *Educational Evaluation and Policy Analysis* 10:237–49.

Gailbraith, James K. 1984. "The Debate about Industrial Policy." In *American Economic Policy: Problems and Prospects,* ed. Gar Alpervitz and Roger Skurski. Notre Dame, IN: Notre Dame University Press.

Gibson, Tom. 1991. "School Choice: The Answer to Education." *Saturday Evening Post,* May/June.

Glenn, Charles L. 1989. "Personal Reflections." In *Choice of Schools in Six Nations*. Washington, DC: U.S. Department of Education.

Goodlad, John. 1984. *A Place Called School*. New York: McGraw-Hill.

Goodsell, Charles T. 1994. *The Case for Bureaucracy*. 3d ed. Chatham, NJ: Chatham House.

Hamilton, Stephen F. 1990. "Apprenticeship in Germany: How Can We Use It Here?" *Harvard Education Letter* 6:1–5.

Hanushek, Erik A. 1981. "Throwing Money at Schools." *Journal of Policy Analysis and Management* 1, 1:19–41.

———. 1986. "The Economics of Schooling: Participation and Performance." *Journal of Economic Literature* 24, 3:1141–77.

Hanushek, Erik A., and Taylor, Lori L. 1990. "Alternative Assessments of the Performance of Schools: Measurement of State Variations in Achievement." *Journal of Human Resources* 25:179–92.

Henig, Jeffrey R. 1994. *Rethinking School Choice*. Princeton, NJ: Princeton University Press.

Hess, Alfred G. 1991. *School Restructuring, Chicago Style*. Newbury Park, CA: Corwin Press.

Hill, Paul T. 1989. *Educational Progress: Cities Mobilize to Improve Their Schools*. Santa Monica, CA: Rand Corporation.

Hirschman, Albert. 1970. *Exit, Choice and Loyalty*. Cambridge: Harvard University Press.

Honig, Bill. 1990–91. "Why Privatizing Education Is a Bad Idea." *Brookings Review*, Winter.

Hsiao, Cheng. 1986. *Analysis of Panel Data*. New York: Cambridge University Press.

Husen, Torsten. 1983. "Are Standards in U.S. Schools Really Lagging Behind Those in Other Countries?" *Phi Delta Kappan* 64:455–61.

Jelier, Richard W. 1993. "Public-Private Partnerships within Public Education in Detroit: Fundamental Reform or Band-Aid Remedies?" Paper presented at the 51st annual meeting of the Midwest Political Science Association. Chicago, April 15–17.

Jencks, C.; Smith, M.; Avery, H.; Bane, M.J.; Cohen, D.; Gintis, J.; Heyns, B.; and Michelson, S. 1972. *Inequality: A Reassessment of the Effect of Family and Schooling in America*. New York: Basic Books.

Judis, John B. 1991. "Why Bush Voucher Plan Would Be a Poor Choice." *In These Times*, September 18–24.

Kozol, Jonathan. 1991. *Savage Inequalities*. New York: Crown.

Lehnen, Robert G. 1992. "Constructing State Education Performance Indicators from ACT and SAT Scores." *Policy Studies Journal* 20, 1:22–40.

Louis, Karen Seashore, and van Velzen, Boudewijn A.M. 1991. "School Choice in the Netherlands." *Educational Leadership* 48:66–72.

Lyons, William E.; and Lowery, David. 1989. "Citizen Responses to Dissatisfaction in Urban Communities: A Partial Test of a General Model." *Journal of Politics* 51:841–68.

Lyons, William E., Lowery, David; and DeHoog, Ruth Hoogland. 1992. *The Politics of Dissatisfaction: Citizens, Services, and Urban Institutions*. Armonk, NY: M.E. Sharpe.

McCubbins, M., Noll, R.; and Weingast, B. 1987. "Administrative Procedures as Instruments of Political Control." *Journal of Law, Economics and Organization*, 3:243–47.

McLean, Martin. 1993. "The Politics of Curriculum in European Perspective." *Educational Review* 45:124–36.

Mazmanian, Daniel A., and Sabatier, Paul A. 1989. *Implementation and Public Policy with a New Postscript.* Washington, DC: National Academy Press.

Meier, Kenneth J., and Smith, Kevin B. 1994. "Representative Democracy and Representative Bureaucracy: Examining the Top Down and the Bottom Up Linkages." *Social Science Quarterly* 75:790–803.

Meier, Kenneth J., and Stewart, Joseph, Jr. 1991. *The Politics of Hispanic Education.* New York: SUNY Press.

Meier, Kenneth J.; Stewart, Joseph, Jr.; and England, Robert E. 1989. *Race, Class and Education: The Politics of Second Generation Discrimination.* Madison: University of Wisconsin Press.

Meyer, Robert H. 1992. "Education Reform: What Constitutes Valid Indicators of Performance?" *La Follette Policy Report* 4, no. 2.

Morgan, David R., and Watson, Sheilah S. 1987. "Comparing Education Performance among the American States." *State and Local Government Review* 19:15–21.

Murphy, Joseph. 1990. "The Education Reform Movement of the 1980s." In *The Educational Reform Movement of the 1980s,* ed. Joseph Murphy. Berkeley: McCutchan.

National Center for Education Statistics, Department of Education. 1992a. *NAEP 1992 Mathematics Report Card for the Nation and the States.* Washington, DC: Government Printing Office.

———. 1992b. *Overview and Inventory of State Requirements for School Coursework and Attendance.* Washington, DC: Government Printing Office.

———. 1992c. *The Condition of Education.* Washington, DC: Government Printing Office.

National Commission on Excellence in Education. 1983. *A Nation at Risk: The Imperative for Educational Reform.* Washington, DC: Government Printing Office.

National Governors' Association. 1986. *Time for Results: The Governors' 1991 Report on Education.* Washington, DC: National Governors' Association.

Niskanen, William A. 1971. *Bureaucracy and Representative Government.* Chicago: Aldine Atherton.

Oakes, Jeannie. 1985. *Keeping Track: How Schools Structure Inequality.* New Haven, CT: Yale University Press.

O'Neill, Barry. 1994. "The History of a Hoax." *New York Times Magazine,* March 6, p. 46.

Payne, Charles. 1991. "The Comer Intervention Model and School Reform in Chicago." *Urban Education* 26:8–24.

Perrow, Charles. 1972. *Complex Organizations.* Glenview, IL: Scott, Foresman.

Peters, T.J., and Waterman, R.H., Jr. 1982. *In Search of Excellence.* New York: Warner Books.

Peterson, Paul E. 1985. *The Politics of School Reform, 1870–1940.* Chicago: University of Chicago Press.

————. 1990. "Monopoly and Competition in American Education." In Clune and Witte, *Choice and Control in American Education.*

Pindyck, Robert S., and Rubinfeld, Daniel L. 1991. *Econometric Models and Econometric Forecasts.* 3d ed. New York: McGraw-Hill.

Powell, Arthur G.; Farrar, Eleanor; and Cohen, David K. 1985. *The Shopping Mall High School: Winners and Losers in the Education Marketplace.* Boston: Houghton Mifflin.

Powell, Brian, and Steelman, Lala Carr. 1984. "Variation in State SAT Performance: Meaningful or Misleading?" *Harvard Educational Review* 54, no. 4:389–412.

Powell, G. Bingham. 1986. "American Voter Turnout in Comparative Perspective." *American Political Science Review* 80:18–43.

Purkey, Stewart C., and Smith, Marshall. 1983. "Effective Schools: A Review." *Elementary School Journal* 83:427–52.

Riley, Dennis D. 1990. "Should Market Forces Control Educational Decision Making?" *American Political Science Review* 84:555–58.

Rodgers, Harrell R., and Bullock, Charles S., III. 1976. *Coercion to Compliance.* Lexington, MA: D.C. Heath.

Rosenholtz, S.J. 1985. "Effective Schools: Interpreting the Evidence." *American Journal of Education* 93:352–88.

Rourke, Francis E. 1984. *Bureaucracy, Politics and Public Policy.* 3d ed. Boston: Little, Brown.

Sandia National Laboratories. 1993. "Perspectives on Education in America: An Annotated Briefing." *Journal of Educational Research* 86:259–310.

Sayrs, Lois W. 1989. *Pooled Time Series Analysis.* Newbury Park, CA: Sage Publications.

Sharkansky, Ira. 1967. "Government Expenditures and Public Service in the American Sates." *American Political Science Review* 61:1066–71.

Simon, Herbert. 1957. *Administrative Behavior: A Study of Decision-Making Processes in Administrative Organization.* New York: Macmillan.

Smith, Kevin B. 1994. "Policy, Markets and Bureaucracy: Reexamining School Choice." *Journal of Politics* 56:475–91.

Smith, Kevin B., and Meier, Kenneth J. 1993. "Politics and the Quality of Education: Policies That Improve Student Performance." Manuscript.

Sosniak, Lauren A., and Ethington, Corinna A. 1992. "When Public School 'Choice' Is Not Academic: Findings from the National Education Longitudinal Study of 1988." *Educational Evaluation and Policy Analysis* 14:33–52.

Stimson, James. 1985. "Regression in Space and Time: A Statistical Essay." *American Journal of Political Science* 29:914–47.

Task Force on Education for Economic Growth. 1983. *Action for Excellence: A Comprehensive Plan to Improve Our Nation's Schools.* Denver: Education Commission of the States.

Thernstrom, Abigail. 1991. "Hobson's Choice." *New Republic,* July 15 and 22.

Thompson, James D. 1967. *Organizations in Action.* New York: McGraw-Hill.

Thurman, W.N., and Fisher, M.E. 1988. "Chickens, Eggs, and Causality, or Which Came First." *American Journal of Agricultural Economics* 70:237–38.

Tiebout, Charles M. 1956. "A Pure Theory of Local Expenditures." *Journal of Political Economy* 64:416–24.

Tweedie, Jack. 1990. "Should Market Forces Control Educational Decision Making?" *American Political Science Review* 84:549–54.

Twentieth Century Fund Task Force on Federal Elementary and Secondary Education Policy. 1983. *Making the Grade: Report.* New York: Twentieth Century Fund.

Tyack, David. 1974. *The One Best System: A History of Urban Education.* Cambridge: Harvard University Press.

———. 1990. "The Public Schools: A Monopoly or a Contested Public Domain?" In Clune and Witte, *Choice and Control in American Education.*

U.S. Department of Education, Office of Educational Research and Improvement. 1988. *Digest of Education Statistics.* Washington, DC: Government Printing Office.

———. 1992a. *Digest of Education Statistics.* Washington, DC: Government Printing Office.

———. 1992b. *Getting Started: How Choice Can Renew Your Public Schools.* Washington, DC: U.S. Government Printing Office.

U.S. House of Representatives Subcommittee on Elementary, Secondary, and Vocational Education. 1990. *Problems Concerning Education Voucher Proposals and Issues Related to Choice.* Washington, DC: Government Printing Office.

"Us and Them." 1989. *Times Educational Supplement,* no. 3806:A19.

Wahlberg, Herbert J., and Rasher, Sue P. 1979. "Achievement in Fifty States." In *Educational Environments and Effects,* ed. Herbert J. Wahlberg. Berkeley, CA: McCutchan.

Wainer, H. 1986. "Five Pitfalls Encountered While Trying to Compare States on Their SAT Scores." *Journal of Educational Measurement* 23, no. 1:69–81.

Weber, Ronald E., and Smith, Kevin B. 1992. "Voter Turnout in U.S. Gubernatorial Elections, 1980–1990: A Pooled Analysis." Paper presented at the annual meeting of the Midwest Political Science Association. Chicago, April 9.

Weiss, Janet A. 1990. "Control in School Organizations: Theoretical Perspectives." In Clune and Witte, *Choice and Control in American Education.*

Whealey, Lois D. 1991. "Choice or Elitism?" *American School Board Journal,* April.

White, Merry. 1987. *The Japanese Educational Challenge.* New York: Free Press.

Wise, A. 1979. *Legislated Learning: The Bureaucratization of the American Classroom.* Berkeley: University of California Press.

Witte, John F. 1990. "Choice and Control: An Analytical Overview." In Clune and Witte, *Choice and Control in American Education.*

———. 1991. "First Year Report on Milwaukee Parental Choice Program." Department of Political Science and Robert M. La Follette Institute of Public Affairs, University of Wisconsin–Madison.

———. 1992. "Private School versus Public School Achievement: Are There Findings That Should Affect the Educational Choice Debate?" *Economics of Education Review* 11:371–94.

Witte, John F.; Bailey, Andrea B.; and Thorn, Christopher A. 1992. "Second Year Report Milwaukee Parental Choice Program." Department of Political Science and Robert M. La Follette Institute of Public Affairs, University of Wisconsin–Madison.

Ziegler, Harmon. 1974. *Governing American Schools: Political Interaction in Local School Districts.* North Scituate, MA: Duxbury Press.

Index

A

Adler, Michael, 26
Ambler, John, 118, 124
American College Testing
    Program (ACT), 84–86, 92n,
    98
    See also Scholastic Aptitude Test
Antoninette (student), 134–35
Arrowhead High School, 3–4
Astin, A., 85

B

Bailey, Andrea, 26
Bainbridge, William, 27
Ball, Stephen, 26, 94, 114, 115, 116,
    117, 127
Belgium, 118
Bennett, William, 1
Best, John, 120
Blalock, Herbert, 68
Bogdan, Kathleen, 136–37, 139
Boswell, John, 27
Bowe, Richard, 26, 94, 114, 115, 116,
    117, 127
Boyer, Eric, 27
Bracey, Gerald, 108, 121, 122
Bridge, Gary, 21
British education system
    centralized bureaucracy, 117
    comparison with United States, 115,
        117
    controversies in, 116–17
    curriculum, 114, 115, 119
    economic consequences of, 108
    education marketplace, 114, 116
    Education Reform Act, 114, 115
    local control, 114, 115, 116
    national standards, 114

British education system *(continued)*
    organization and institutional
        structure, 114–15, 116
    school choice, 114, 117, 118
    school closures, 116
Brown, Byron, 66, 94, 124, 126
Bruce Guadalupe Community School,
    10–12, 14n
Bryk, Anthony, 21, 77, 94
Bullock, Charles, 67
Bureaucracy
    in Britain, 117
    causes of, 40–41, 57, 59
    definitions of, 25, 40–41
    effects on performance, 30n, 38, 39,
        40–41, 51, 59–60, 96–97,
        102–3
    in Japan, 112–13
    operationalization of, 51–52, 100,
        128–29
    red tape, 40
Bush, George, 33

C

Canada, 118
Carnegie Foundation, 26, 27, 30n, 33,
    35, 66, 94, 126
Carr, Robert, 27
Castellanos, Vicente, 10–11
Catholic and parochial schools
    effectiveness of, 3, 5–6
    enrollment, 63n, 69, 71–72
    history, 5
    in Milwaukee, 5
    parental involvement in, 5
    religious instruction, 66
    school choice participation, 5–6, 9,
        13, 127
    student opinions in, 6–7, 9

—————— About the Authors ——————

Kevin B. Smith is Assistant Professor of Political Science snd Public Administration at the University of Nebraska–Lincoln.

Kenneth J. Meier is Professor of Political Science at the University of Wisconsin–Milwaukee and Editor of the *American Journal of Political Science.*